COMPETITIVE BIDDING WITH TWO SUITED HANDS

by
MAX HARDY

Published by
DEVYN PRESS, INC.
Louisville, Kentucy

OTHER BOOKS BY MAX HARDY

Five Card Majors — Western Style 1974 (out of print — replaced by Two-Over-One Game Force)
Play My Card (with Bill Roney) 1980 (out of print)
Two Over One Game Force 1982 (original — out of print — replaced by Two-Over-One Game Force — Revised and Expanded)
New Minor Forcing (out of print) 1984
Fourth Suit Forcing 1984
Forcing Notrump Responses (out of print) 1984
Modern Bidding Tools 1984
Splinters and Other Shortness Bids 1987
Two Over One Game Force — Revised and Expanded 1989
Two Over One Game Force: An Introduction (with Steve Bruno)
Two Over One Game Force Quiz Book 1993
The Problems With Major Suit Raises 1998

First Printing — April 1996
Second Printing — July 1999

Printed in the United States of America.

Published by
Devyn Press, Inc.
3600 Chamberlain Lane, Suite 230
Louisville, KY 40241
1-800-274-2221

ISBN No. 0-939460-57-2

INTRODUCTION

Most of the books that I have written were intended to be textbooks. My purpose was to present methods already accepted as viable and used by successful players, so that the student of the game could have a reliable reference source. History indicates that I have succeeded in fulfilling my purpose. My textbooks have been well received and widely read. I have been acknowledged as the "Guru" of the bidding methods known as "Two Over One — Game Force." For this, I must register my appreciation of the acceptance of my efforts by those who have purchased and read my books.

My most recent efforts have been directed toward a different objective. I have noted several situations in which even the expert community has become lax and lazy. Rather than question methods which might not be serving their purpose — that of attaining optimum exchange of information in any auction — the majority of today's most frequent and successful competitors in the duplicate bridge arena woodenly accept methods which are used by the majority. Since everybody follows the leader, when situations arise which require tools which will solve problems, nearly all of the field is similarly inadequately prepared. Using the same unquestioned methods, all have an equal shot at solving the problem at hand, and only the most thoughtful or ingenious will be able to provide a better solution than the rest of the masses.

My own methods attempt to address these problems that I have determined are real, but ignored. Although I have mentioned these methods in my textbooks, until now I have not stressed the obvious problem. I have not preached the need to solve unaddressed situations nor thrust my own solutions upon any but my own students. In this book, I do address inadequacies in standard methods for bidding competitively with certain two-suited hands. In future books, I hope to carry forward my campaign to educate those who are willing to study other methods which are far more valuable than the accepted tools.

This book breaks ground in an important direction for me. I hope that the reader will appreciate my attempt to furnish superior tools which I believe do solve problems which have been previously ignored. When time permits, I hope to address other situations which I believe are similar — those in which the world woodenly accepts certain tools which I believe do not adequately solve certain important bidding problems.

I hope that the reader will appreciate my efforts in this presentation. If my fondest hopes are realized, I will note the methods presented here in use by many of my opponents when I am able to play in the competitive arena.

Max Hardy
Las Vegas, Nevada
March 1996

TABLE OF CONTENTS

PART THREE — TWO-SUITED DEFENSES

PART ONE

BIDDING COMPETITIVELY WITH UNEVEN TWO SUITED HANDS

CHAPTER ONE
DESCRIBING THE PROBLEM

When your opponents have opened the bidding and you have the desire to compete, there are many types of hands that may suggest you take action. With opening bid values and support for all of the unbid suits, you might make a takeout double. With a strong suit of your own, you might overcall. To show a specific type of hand that has been previously agreed, you might make a cue bid.

Although there are methods that are traditionally used to show many of the types of hands when you may wish to compete, one hand type suffers from acute neglect. When one holds a hand of this particular type, he has no available methods to indicate the nature of his hand. This hand type is the two suiter in which the suits to be shown are not equal in length.

When the longer and/or stronger suit is a major suit, it is relatively easy to bid that major suit, even at the risk of losing a possible fit in the shorter or weaker minor suit. By overcalling first in the major suit, and perhaps introducing the minor suit later, one can emphasize the major suit which is the desired description.

When the minor suit is longer or stronger, the bidder has the choice of overcalling in that minor suit and perhaps losing a fit in the major, or distorting what he wants to describe by bidding the shorter or weaker major suit first. Facing this dilemma, one can only hope to guess correctly which action will succeed on a specific occasion.

To illustrate this problem and its lack of solution, consider the following. It is problem A from the Master Solvers' Club of the *Bridge World*, the November 1993 issue.

IMPs, none vul. You, South hold:

♠ K6 ♥ AJ105 ♦ Q2 ♣ KQ986

South	West	North	East
		Pass	1♦
?			

What call do you make?

The experts on the panel are required to use Bridge World Standard in presenting their answers, but may offer various thoughts regarding a preferred method. Apparently, none of the twenty-eight experts who offered their answers and their thoughts recognized that perhaps instead of taking a shot at an action that would have the best chance of success, one should have some systemic tool available to express this type of hand.

Moderator Eric Kokish assigned scores for the various guesses as follows:

Action	Score	Votes	Solvers
1♥	100	16	39
2♣	70	7	37
Pass	60	1	3
Double	50	2	16
1NT	50	2	5

Certainly, the action to receive the top score of 100 should be a call which says, "Partner, I have a hand with hearts and clubs, but my clubs are either longer or stronger than my hearts."

To document the frequency with which the uneven two suited hands occur, we picked up the hand printouts from five sessions at a Regional Tournament. Glancing through these printouts, we discovered more than thirty hands which fit the general description. We then posed the problem of describing each of these hands if an opening bid in one of the two remaining suits had been made by an opponent.

Here are the example hands.

1. ♠ J943
   ♥ J98
   ♦ 4
   ♣ AK854

White against red you may wish to compete against a one heart opening bid. Can you show clubs and still suggest spades?

2. ♠ —
   ♥ 9865
   ♦ AQJ92
   ♣ KQ98

When the opening bid is one spade, you can make a takeout double. What do you do when the opening bid is one club?

3. ♠ 73
   ♥ K652
   ♦ Q
   ♣ QJ8643

At favorable vulnerability you might like to stir up some action. What do you do when the opening bid is one spade? Or one diamond?

4. ♠ AQ108
   ♥ A102
   ♦ J
   ♣ AK1063

When the opening bid is one diamond, a takeout double will work. What if the opening bid is one heart?

5.   ♠ K1043
      ♥ 3
      ♦ 54
      ♣ AJ9632

What do you do after an opening bid in either red suit?

6.   ♠ K983
      ♥ A53
      ♦ KJ10652
      ♣ —

The opening bid is one heart. How do you compete?

7.   ♠ KJ
      ♥ A1064
      ♦ AKQ93
      ♣ 54

How do you compete against an opening bid in either black suit?

8.   ♠ J9742
      ♥ 2
      ♦ 94
      ♣ KQ985

At favorable, they open with a red suit. What do you do?

9.   ♠ Q
      ♥ 98652
      ♦ A9
      ♣ AKJ107

They open either spades or diamonds. How do you compete?

10. ♠ 8
    ♥ AKQ4
    ♦ 1094
    ♣ AQ432

They again open in either spades or diamonds. Your turn?

11. ♠ AJ42
    ♥ 42
    ♦ AJ865
    ♣ A4

They open either one club or one heart. Your call?

12. ♠ K743
    ♥ AQ
    ♦ AKJ106
    ♣ J5

They open with one club or one heart. What do you do?

13. ♠ KQ86
    ♥ 9
    ♦ Q43
    ♣ AK1094

They open in a red suit. How do you compete?

14. ♠ 103
    ♥ K864
    ♦ J8
    ♣ KQJ105

They open with either one spade or one diamond. What do you do?

15. ♠ Q93
    ♥ AQ86
    ♦ 3
    ♣ AQ873

Against one diamond you can make a takeout double. What if they open with one spade?

16. ♠ 752
    ♥ KQ82
    ♦ 4
    ♣ AK1093

Similar to the previous problem, but your spades are too poor for a takeout double of one diamond. How do you compete?

17. ♠ 74
    ♥ AQJ7
    ♦ 54
    ♣ A10852

How do you compete after an opening bid of either one spade or one diamond?

18. ♠ AQ954
    ♥ 3
    ♦ 10
    ♣ AKQ1082

When the opening bid is in a red suit, how do you compete?

19. ♠ AQ102
    ♥ 3
    ♦ Q9863
    ♣ KQ9

You can make a takeout double of a one heart opening bid. But what if the opening bid is one club?

20. ♠ AJ82
    ♥ A83
    ♦ Q
    ♣ AJ985

The theme continues. Against one diamond you can double. What if they open with one heart?

21. ♠ 4
    ♥ A1094
    ♦ Q10
    ♣ AJ10632

They open with one spade or one diamond. What do you do?

22. ♠ Q8652
    ♥ AK
    ♦ 4
    ♣ AJ865

They open in either red suit. What call do you make?

23. ♠ AK105
    ♥ —
    ♦ A832
    ♣ AK1043

You can double one heart, but what about one diamond?

24. ♠ K7
    ♥ AK98
    ♦ 53
    ♣ QJ652

They open with one spade or one diamond. Your choice?

25. ♠ QJ73
    ♥ 7
    ♦ Q76
    ♣ AKJ106

You can double one heart, but what about one diamond?

26. ♠ Q
    ♥ QJ64
    ♦ A6
    ♣ A108743

How do you compete against one spade or one diamond?

27. ♠ Q8652
    ♥ A5
    ♦ Q
    ♣ AK654

They open in a red suit. Your turn?

28. ♠ AQ62
    ♥ 10
    ♦ 862
    ♣ KQ973

Same question. Your answer?

29. ♠ 75
     ♥ Q983
     ♦ AJ
     ♣ A10542

Against one spade or one diamond, how do you compete?

30. ♠ A6532
     ♥ K
     ♦ KJ9875
     ♣ 6

Against one heart you can use Michaels. What do you do over one club?

These are not all of the hands from the five sheets and these are not hands created to prove a point. They happen again and again. And the methods popularly in use today cannot solve the problems.

We have asked how you would bid each of these hands when the opening bid by the opposing side has been in one of your shorter suits. If the opening bid is in one of your two longest suits, might it also be right to enter the auction?

When the opening bid is in your four card suit, an overcall in your longer (stronger) five or six card suit becomes even more attractive. Partner is likely to be short in your second suit, allowing you to ruff losers in that suit in the dummy he will present.

But what if the opening bid is in your longer suit? Are you now kept completely out of the auction? Or are there some hands when competition is still appropriate? And if so, by what method do you get into the auction?

In the pages that follow we will present an integrated competitive bidding approach which, if adopted in its entirety, will allow your partnership to bid these problem hands. The methods described and suggested will require you to assign a different meaning to your use of cue bids, to incorporate an additional type of takeout double into your arsenal, and to make certain jump overcalls conventional. If you undertake to use this integrated bidding package, you will have found solutions for bidding this type of hand. We believe that you will appreciate the improvement in your results when this type of problem needs to be solved.

CHAPTER TWO
CUE BIDS

Historically, the use of a Cue Bid in the opponents' suit as an entry into the auction has undergone great metamorphosis during the past three decades. During the fifties and early sixties, the use generally assigned to the Cue Bid was a hand of great playing strength, usually with first or second round control and shortness in the suit that had been bid by the opponents. Charles Goren had set this meaning for the direct Cue Bid, and at that time his methods were considered to be the accepted standard.

The problem with this assigned usage for the Cue Bid was one of frequency. When the bidding had been opened by the opposing side, one rarely held the hand that would be shown by this assigned use of a Cue Bid of the opponents' suit.

Prior to his untimely death in 1966, Mike Michaels undertook to establish a different assigned use for the Cue Bid. He suggested that the Cue Bid be used to show a weak two suited hand, usually five-five in distribution, and in the range of about six to eleven high card points. When the opening bid had been a minor suit, the Cue Bid showed both majors; if the opening bid had been in a major suit, the Cue Bid showed the other major and one of the minors. When the Advancer had no fit for the known major suit and needed to know which minor suit was in the hand of the Cue Bidder, his call of two notrump would ask the Cue Bidder to indicate which of the minor suits he held.

The Michaels Cue Bid caught on instantly in the world of competitive duplicate bridge. It became one of those conventions that virtually everyone played. For more than two decades, duplicate players have woodenly included Michaels Cue Bids as part of their partnership agreements without any further examination of that tool to determine whether it has been solving the problem of bidding difficult hands. Certainly, if another easy method can be employed to show those two suited hands that are five-five in distribution and in the range of six to eleven high card points, the Cue Bid might be released to another, more useful, function.

The contention here is that the hands currently being shown by the use of the Michaels Cue Bid can be bid just as readily by the use of other methods (which will be presented and discussed fully). The meaning assigned to the use of a Cue Bid in the suit of the opening bidder could best be used to solve the problem of bidding truly difficult hands.

By finding an easy alternate way of bidding Michaels hands, we can release the use of the Cue Bid of the opener's suit to solve part of the problem expressed in Chapter One. We will assign to the Cue Bid conveyance of the message that the bidder holds the problem hand which consists of two suits, a longer or stronger (or both) minor suit, and a shorter or weaker (or both) major suit. If the Cue Bid can send a message of this hand type and also indicate which suits the bidder holds, it will solve one of the problems that has been discussed.

THE TOP AND BOTTOM CUE BID

The leading authoritative sources indicate that information regarding the Top and Bottom Cue Bid has largely been ignored. In the *Official Encyclopedia of Bridge, Fifth Edition,* this is the total reference: "TOP AND BOTTOM CUEBID. An immediate overcall in the opponent's major suit to show the highest and lowest ranking unbid suits. See also MICHAELS CUEBID." One would expect this primary source to give some real information about such an important tool. However, the world has so completely accepted Michaels without question that what should be a definitive presentation about Top and Bottom is not. Reference to the convention is quite perfunctory, and the enquirer is referred to the accepted tool rather than given information which would allow him to make a reasonable choice between available methods. The brief reference is not even accurate, since the Top and Bottom Cue Bid is not necessarily limited to the Cue Bid of an opponent's major suit, but may be made after an opposing opening bid in any suit.

In *Bridge Conventions Complete,* in the short presentation on Top and Bottom Cue Bids, author Amalya Kearse briefly tells what suits are shown by each Cue Bid, then points out that Top and Bottom cannot be used to show both major suits, and advises the reader to use Michaels over minor suit opening bids. It is further pointed out that if Top and Bottom Cue Bids are used only over majors, the convention will never show a two suiter that includes diamonds. Once again the prejudice for Michaels is noted.

In *Modern Bridge Conventions* by Root and Pavlicek, the prejudice is even more strongly apparent. Although a complete presentation on Michaels is made, Top and Bottom Cue Bids are not even mentioned.

As the first step in solving the problem under discussion, the Cue Bid of the opening bidder's suit shows the highest and lowest ranking of the remaining suits, and suggests that the lowest suit is longer or stronger (or both) than the major suit which is also being indicated. When the advancer has a moderate hand with marginal fits for both suits, he is advised to bid the lower ranking of the two suits shown by the Cue Bid. When he has a good fit for the higher of the two suits, he is happy to bid that suit, with knowledge that not only is a major suit fit available, but that there will also be an additional source of tricks in the minor suit shown by the Cue Bidder.

When the opening bid is one club, the Cue Bid shows diamonds and spades with the diamond suit expected to be longer or stronger (or both) than the spade suit. The Cue Bidder typically holds five or six diamonds and four spades. When he has a fifth spade, his spade suit will be so poor that an overcall in his five card suit instead of a Cue Bid would be a poor description of the two suits that he holds.

When the opening bid is either red suit, the Top and Bottom Cue Bid shows clubs and spades, with the emphasis again on the lower ranking suit of the two. Since this application covers opening bids in two of the four suits, half of the uses of Top and Bottom Cue Bids will be in situations when the suits shown by the Cue Bid are clubs and spades.

When the opening bid is one spade, the Top and Bottom Cue Bid shows clubs and hearts with longer or stronger (or both) clubs than hearts.

You should notice that in all possible situations, the use of the Top and Bottom Cue Bid will show one of the black suits. Only when the opening bid is spades does the Cue Bid show hearts as the highest ranking unbid suit. Only when the opening bid is clubs does the Cue Bid show diamonds as the lowest ranking unbid suit. Therefore, most examples will concentrate on an auction in which the black suits are shown by a Top and Bottom Cue Bid. But the reader should be aware that many auctions which begin with a black suit bid by the opposition will create a shift, causing hearts to be the top suit, or diamonds to become the bottom suit.

Since the lower of the two suits expressed by the Top and Bottom Cue Bid is always expected to be longer or stronger (or both) than the higher of the two suits shown, the Advancer will consider the lower ranking suit to be a safe haven when he has marginal fits for the two suits that have been indicated. Holding doubletons in both suits, Advancer will prefer the lower ranking suit routinely. Holding three cards in the upper suit and a singleton or void in the lower suit, Advancer should prefer the upper suit, expecting that in most instances he is opting for a three-four fit, knowing that the lower suit could easily be six cards in length.

The strength range for the Cue Bid itself is dictated by the conditions of play. At matchpoints the requirements for the Cue Bid relate to the tactical situation at hand. When you wish to give your opponents a problem and hold a hand of the required distribution, if the vulnerability is favorable and your partner is a passed hand, use your imagination!! At IMPs or when partner has not yet passed, your decision should be based on what partner should expect from you at the given vulnerability. Since the minor suit should provide a source of tricks whether it is the trump suit or not, imposition of a high card requirement should not infringe on the use of judgment.

Knowing the minimum strength for the given situation, considering both distribution and high cards, when Advancer senses the possibility of a game in the upper suit, he can jump in that suit to invite, or simply bid the indicated major suit game. If Advancer jumps in the lower suit, he will usually bypass the opportunity to play game in notrump. For this reason, a jump in the lower suit should carry the implication not of strength, but of a good fit and the need to preempt in order to create maximum pressure on the opponents. When Advancer does have good values but no fit for the upper suit, he can make another Cue Bid in the suit of the opponents to find out how good the hand of the Cue Bidder is, relative to the conditions of play.

If the Advancer, having heard the Top and Bottom call, bids in the remaining suit, he indicates that his own suit is self sufficient and that he has no interest in playing in either suit shown by the Cue Bid. Armed with an understanding of this particular auction, when the Cue Bidder holds a fit for the suit shown by the Advancer, his hand may grow enough in value to justify a raise of the Advancer's known good suit. Here, fits and controls could produce a game or even a slam in the Advancer's suit, with very little in high cards.

Most Top and Bottom Cue Bid auctions will be rather mundane. Having described his hand's distribution and heard Advancer bid one of the shown suits cheaply (usually the lower ranking one), the Cue Bidder will rarely have reason to bid again.

If Advancer bids cheaply in the upper suit, knowing about the fit may enable the Cue Bidder to either invite or bid a game when he holds reasonable values. Knowledge of the fit in his shorter (major) suit can be the impetus to get the bidder's side to a game based upon that fit supplemented by the side source of tricks in the longer and stronger minor suit.

This type of auction is similar to an uncontested situation when the opening bidder, holding a good six-four hand, might have used the conventional approach known as the Six-Four Fragment. When an opening bidder has bid a good six card minor suit and has a four card fit for the major suit of the Responder, he conventionally rebids by jumping to the four level in his minor suit. This indicates a four card fit for Responder's major suit as well as a side source of tricks. In such an auction, when Responder learns the nature of opener's hand, he will know when it is right to pursue a fitting slam, and when it is right to subside. When a Top and Bottom Cue Bid has been used, and Advancer bids the top suit and the Cue Bidder raises, he should hold the same type of hand that would have induced the use of a Six-Four Fragment if the Cue Bidder had instead been an opening bidder.

The Cue Bidder does not, however, have license to force the auction to game in his upper four card suit just because Advancer has elected to bid that suit. The Cue Bidder must remember the difference between the situation in which his four card suit has been bid by a Responder as opposed to an Advancer. A Responder who is selecting his call freely will certainly hold four or more cards in the upper suit, and a fit of at least eight cards is guaranteed. When instead it is an Advancer who bids the upper suit, it is possible that he has bid a three card suit, selecting between the two suits shown by the Cue Bid when he holds a singleton or void in the lower suit.

Another possible auction is one in which Advancer has bid cheaply in the lower ranking suit shown by the Top and Bottom Cue Bid. If the Cue Bidder next voluntarily bids the Top suit which he has already indicated with his Cue Bid, he shows a massive hand. The voluntary introduction of his higher ranking suit which was not selected by his partner indicates that both suits are at least five cards long, and that the Cue Bid was based on a very good hand. With this information when the Advancer has an appropriate hand, he can bid a game or even suggest a slam, knowing that he has the right cards to augment the excellent hand his partner, the Cue Bidder, has shown.

Now let us look at some example hands and auctions utilizing Top and Bottom Cue Bids.

♠ 84	♠ AJ73	♠ AJ73
♥ AJ73	♥ 84	♥ 84
♦ 6	♦ KQ10954	♦ 6
♣ KQ10954	♣ 6	♣ KQ10954

These three hands are actually the same hand, presented three times with different major/minor configurations. In the first presentation when the opposing opening bid is one spade, of the remaining suits hearts is the Top suit and clubs is the Bottom suit. Against a one spade opening bid this is a typical Top and Bottom Cue Bid.

In the second presentation of the example hand, when the opening bid is one club, spades is the Top suit and diamonds is the Bottom suit. This hand also will be described by a Top and Bottom Cue Bid.

In the third presentation of this hand, when the opening bid is in either red suit, spades is the Top suit and clubs is the Bottom suit. Make a Top and Bottom Cue Bid against an opening bid of either one diamond or one heart.

♠ 108643
♥ 7
♦ K5
♣ AKQ108

In this example the black suits are even in quantity, but certainly not even in quality. After an opposing opening bid of either one diamond or one heart, if the black suits were inverted, one should be quite happy to overcall in the excellent spade suit and not worry about losing a possible fit in the poor club suit. Given the opportunity to bid the poor club suit later if partner had not shown a spade fit, one would most probably do so.

However, in the example the problem is quite different. The message we are sending to partner is that we have uneven suits with a greater desire to play in clubs than spades. However, we want him to keep spades in the picture so that when he has a fit for spades he will be encouraged to bid that suit. Were we to overcall in spades we would expect partner to raise on any three card holding, or even a doubleton honor, which could lead to disaster.

When the auction continues and the opponents declare either in a red suit or in notrump, we would certainly want a club lead, not a spade lead. We cannot send the proper message to partner by overcalling in the very poor spade suit even though it is five cards long. Here is another situation where the Top and Bottom Cue Bid gives partner the best information.

♠ AKJ75
♥ A4
♦ 8
♣ KQJ103

Against an opening bid in either red suit, using today's standard methods, it is almost impossible to bid this hand accurately. When the opening bid is one heart and we overcall one spade, we may languish short of game. If we make a takeout double and partner does not respond in spades, when we bid spades at our next turn we paint a picture of a much more substantial suit. This could eventually cause us to play in an inferior fit at a high level. If we make a Michaels Cue Bid showing spades and a minor suit (admittedly out of the expected range, but often still the choice of Michaels practitioners), partner will often bid two notrump to ask for the minor suit and our means of describing this hand will not be at all adequate.

When the opening bid is one diamond there are similar problems. If we overcall in spades, we will likely languish short of game when partner's meager values are adequate to produce a game facing this excellent hand. If we make a takeout double and partner jumps to game in hearts, four spades will appear to be a Cue Bid in support of hearts rather than a real suit (or it might be Kickback - RKC in hearts!!)

When your agreement is to use Top and Bottom Cue Bids, this hand is easy to describe. You begin by making that Cue Bid after the opponents have opened in either red suit. If Advancer, as expected, bids cheaply in clubs, when you next bid spades you show a hand that has enough strength to make a game facing almost no values, and you also show at least five-five distribution in spades and clubs. On the rare occasion where Advancer bids spades rather than clubs, this hand can next jump to four diamonds. This is a splinter bid showing enough values to play four spades facing nothing but spade length, and also indicating interest in a slam and shortness in diamonds.

♠ Q4
♥ J743
♦ A8732
♣ 93

After an opening bid of one heart (or one diamond) you have heard partner make a Top and Bottom Cue Bid. You expect that his clubs are longer or stronger (or both) than his spades. You routinely bid three clubs, selecting the known "anchor" suit without in any way encouraging your partner to move forward.

♠ Q42
♥ J743
♦ A873
♣ 93

This is almost the same hand, but it has one more spade than the previous example. Here it is still correct to bid clubs rather than spades. Partner will often hold six clubs, but even when he only holds a five card club suit, the quality of that suit should be such that the opponents cannot have good enough trumps to try to punish you at the three level in your five-two fit. It would be wrong to bid spades just because you hold three of that suit. Partner usually holds only four in the Top suit, but when he hears you bid that suit he may be encouraged to take further action, expecting you to hold four cards in the spade suit. Look to the hand above where the Cue Bidder holds five bad spades. Holding that hand, if he made a Cue Bid and heard Advancer bid in spades, he might easily decide to raise thinking that a possible five-four existed and that a fitting game is likely.

♠ Q42
♥ J743
♦ A8732
♣ 9

This third similar hand should make the Advancer uncomfortable. Here since he holds only a singleton club and three spades to an honor, he has little choice but to bid spades. He is aware that when the Cue Bidder hears him bid in the upper suit, he may push toward a possible game, hoping for a four card fit. However, to select what might be a five-one fit by bidding clubs would not be a good idea.

♠ Q1042
♥ 86
♦ AQ754
♣ K3

When this Advancer hears a Top and Bottom Cue Bid of an opening red suit, he should visualize the possibility of a game in spades. When he is a passed hand, and when the vulnerability is favorable, he should be cautious since his partner may be taking liberties. A jump to three spades will invite a game, which is just about right for this hand. If Advancer is unpassed or if his side is vulnerable, Advancer should feel comfortable jumping to four spades with this hand.

♠ Q10432
♥ 6
♦ AQ754
♣ K3

When the opening bid is one diamond and partner has made a Top and Bottom Cue Bid, a return Cue Bid of three diamonds should indicate an interest not only in playing game, but some thought of slam as well. When the opening bid is one heart, after partner's Top and Bottom Cue Bid the Advancer can splinter by jumping to four hearts. The splinter would not be possible after an opening bid of one diamond, since in that auction a jump to four hearts should be natural.

♠ KQ85
♥ 6
♦ AK963
♣ A104

You would not expect to hold a hand this good and hear an opening bid in a red suit followed by a Top and Bottom Cue Bid from partner. When partner has as much as ace fourth of spades and the king-queen fifth of clubs, a spade slam should be easy. If in addition partner holds the heart ace, a grand should be bid. Start by making a return Cue Bid, then ask for key cards. Since partner is known to hold a two suited hand, in key card auctions both suits are included. When partner shows three key cards you can then ask for queens in the key suits. In such auctions queens should be shown or denied in steps: the first step denies both queens, the second step shows the queen of the lower suit, the third step shows the queen of the upper suit, the fourth step shows both queens. When partner holds the club queen the grand will be cold except when partner's shape is 4-1-3-5. It's worth that risk.

♠ Q5
♥ AQJ10865
♦ 843
♣ 6

After an opening bid of one diamond, you have heard a Top and Bottom Cue Bid from partner. Although partner has shown clubs and spades, you have no desire to play in either of those suits since your own good suit should certainly be the trump suit. You will bid hearts at the level indicated by the vulnerability. If not vulnerable, just bid two hearts; if vulnerable, you can expect more values from partner and a jump to three hearts is justified. If your diamonds and clubs were interchanged, you should jump to four hearts at any vulnerability.

♠ J62
♥ KQ76
♦ AQ98
♣ Q4

Again partner has made a Cue Bid after an opposing opening bid in one of the red suits. Bid two notrump if not vulnerable, but if vulnerable, bid three notrump. When your side is not vulnerable and your partner has extra values beyond what he needed at that vulnerability to use the Top and Bottom convention, he will carry on to three notrump.

♠ 8
♥ 10932
♦ K1054
♣ Q753

When partner has made a Top and Bottom Cue Bid after an opening bid in either red suit, it is clear that the opponents are likely to have eight spades between them, but they may not be able to find their fit. It is also clear that they probably have the values for a game, with at least one of them short in clubs, since partner holds five or six cards in that suit. A preemptive raise to four clubs may easily cause the bad guys to play in the wrong suit, or to sell out and defend four clubs which is likely to be to our advantage.

♠ AQ108
♥ 4
♦ 63
♣ KQ10854

About twenty years ago a friend of mine gave me this hand and presented an interesting problem. He held this hand vulnerable in first position against not vulnerable opponents. He told me that as he prepared to open the bidding with one club, his left hand opponent bid four hearts out of turn. His partner declined to accept the out of turn call, so he again was posed with opening the bidding, knowing that whatever he bid the next call would be four hearts on his left. He thought about opening with one club and next bidding four spades over the anticipated four heart overcall, but had strong reservations, since if the hand belonged to the opponents, his bid of four spades might volunteer for a large penalty. He asked what I would have done.

My answer was that I would open the bidding with one heart!!!! In my partnerships we have agreed to play Top and Bottom Cue Bids. Considering that we both knew that the next call would be four hearts, my opening bid was a Cue Bid, showing six clubs and four spades. This information would allow partner to make an informed choice. I would not have to guess what to do if I opened one club and was then faced with a decision over the anticipated bid of four hearts followed by two passes. I think that this incident might give new meaning to the term, "Advance Cue Bid."

CHAPTER THREE
CONVENTIONAL JUMP OVERCALLS

In Chapter Two we dealt with situations in which the uneven suits were the highest and lowest of the remaining suits, excluding the suit of the opening bid. On most occasions, the top suit was spades. Only when the opening bid was in spades did hearts become the top suit. The same hand type can be found in another common configuration, when the opening bid is one minor suit and the suits held by the defensive bidder are the other minor and hearts. With spades as the suit we do not want to show, we cannot make use of a Top and Bottom Cue Bid. Instead, the suits we wish to show are the two lower ranking of the three remaining suits. To achieve this description, we make a descriptive conventional jump overcall.

When the opening bid is clubs and we hold diamonds and hearts with suits that are even in length, it is easy to overcall in hearts and plan to bid diamonds later, or without defensive strength, use the Unusual Notrump. However, the problem hand again is the one in which the suits are uneven in length. Hands with only four hearts and a five or six card diamond suit, or five-five with excellent diamonds and very poor hearts, need a descriptive call similar to the Top and Bottom Cue Bid. We indicate a hand of this nature after an opposing bid of one club by jumping to two diamonds. Systemically, this jump overcall shows diamonds and hearts, with the emphasis on diamonds.

Similarly, when the opening bid is one diamond and we hold clubs and hearts, if the heart suit is five cards and of good quality, we would have no objection to overcalling in hearts, even at the possible expense of losing the club suit. But when the hearts are only four cards long and clubs are a good five or six card suit, we need a way to show this disparity without losing either suit. To describe this particular hand after the opening bid of one diamond, we make a conventional jump overcall of three clubs.

Again, this auction places emphasis on clubs, with a shorter or much weaker heart suit.

The test of the viability of any convention comes from the comparrison of what you receive from its use, as opposed to what you give up to be able to use the convention. Currently, most of us are committed to the use of preemptive single jump overcalls. In order to incorporate the two special conventional jump overcalls explained above into our systemic agreements, we would need to give up a jump to two diamonds over an opening bid of one club as preemptive, and also give up the preemptive jump overcall of three clubs after an opening bid of one diamond.

When the opening bid is one club, a jump to two diamonds usually does very little in the way of disruption. If the hand has a good diamond suit that warrants preemption, the tactical call of three diamonds will clearly be much more effective. Giving up the preemptive jump to two diamonds to the conventional application that shows diamonds and hearts with longer or stronger (or both) diamonds is almost no loss at all.

Giving up the preemptive jump to three clubs after an opening bid of one diamond is another matter. This particular preempt is quite effective since it prevents establishment of a major suit fit at both the one and two levels when the opponents might otherwise be able to find such a fit. In order to use this particular call as a conventional bid showing an uneven hand with clubs and hearts, the price is more substantial.

All considered, the pros for the use of these two conventional jumps appear to have the edge over the cons. The major drawback in adopting these conventional jumps appears to be the usual problem, that of memory. When it becomes ingrained to use a call for a certain purpose and when a different meaning is assigned to the use of that call, you will possibly forget and make the call with a hand that once was appropriate before the meaning of the call was changed. The good news is that even if you or your partner forget, you will at least settle into your longest and strongest suit.

Here are a few examples.

♠ J5
♥ AQ86
♦ KJ9543
♣ 7

This hand is typical for the jump to two diamonds after an opening bid of one club.

♠ K6
♥ AJ105
♦ Q2
♣ KQ986

Once again we see Problem A from the Bridge World Master Solvers Club, November 1993. When the opposing opening bid is one diamond, wouldn't you rather to jump to three clubs to describe this hand than have to guess to bid one heart? Or two clubs? Or Pass, double, or one notrump?

This use of conventional jump overcalls to describe a two suited hand with a shorter or weaker heart suit and a longer and/ or stronger holding in the unbid minor suit when the opponents have opened in a minor suit is part of a complete system. When adopted in its entirety, this will allow a partnership to describe any such hand comfortably.

CHAPTER IV
TAKEOUT DOUBLES

We are going to attempt to classify and label takeout doubles of several varieties. We doubt that this has been done before. When a bridge player thinks about what a takeout double is, his thinking is usually of the most common variety of takeout double.

We believe that there are four separate and distinct types of takeout doubles that are used in bridge today. Two of these types are used by nearly everyone who plays the game, without thought of classifying them separately.

TAKEOUT DOUBLES — TYPE I

Type one is the classic takeout double. After an opening bid by an opponent, the defensive bidder makes a double which shows about the values of an opening bid or more and indicates support for all of the unbid suits. If the doubler's values are minimum — just about opening bid strength — he does not voluntarily bid again. If the response to his takeout double is forcing, or if it is highly invitational and he has a smidgeon extra, it is considered right for him to bid again. If the Advancer merely selects a suit from among those offered by the takeout double, the doubler does not bid again unless he has substantial extra values beyond those shown by the original takeout double.

A common bidding error by inexperienced players is making a takeout double without support for one of the unbid suits. When the Advancer names that short suit, the doubler who does not understand the language believes that he can then correct to a suit of his own, or to notrump. He doesn't comprehend in any way that when he takes this action, he has described a completely different hand. What he has done is indicate that he holds a Type II takeout double.

TAKEOUT DOUBLES — TYPE II

There are times that you wish to compete by overcalling in a very good suit, or by overcalling in notrump, but the hand you hold is too good for that action. With a balanced nineteen count, if you overcall by bidding one notrump, partner will not move forward holding a seven count, and a game which should be bid will be missed. Similarly, when you hold an excellent suit of six or seven cards and good high card values (something in the neighborhood of a seventeen or eighteen count in high cards) if you overcall in your good suit, partner will have no clue that meager values are all that might be needed to produce a game.

Whenever the defensive bidder has a hand that seems just too good for an overcall because of the danger of missing a game, he begins by making a Type II takeout double. When he later bids either in his own good suit, or in notrump, his message is that he did not have a Type I takeout double with support for all of the unbid suits. Instead his hand was oriented to a single suit or to notrump, and that he held values that were too good to allow him to just overcall at his previous turn.

TAKEOUT DOUBLES — TYPE III

This third type should really not be called a takeout double, for its function is not to ask Advancer to select a suit. Used by the Italian Blue team (who were fully aware of what they were doing), this double had the simple purpose of announcing the values of an opening bid. Support for unbid suits was not even suggested and the Advancer might have to feel his way to a playable contract, but he did so armed with the knowledge that his partner did, in fact, hold the values of an opening bid.

Many people who attempt to play bridge (and are not at all aware of what they are doing) similarly use what they call a takeout double for this sole purpose — to show the values of an opening bid. They often encounter problems in competitive duplicate play for their use of this approach is a departure from standard bidding and THEY ARE COMPLETELY UNA-

WARE OF THIS FACT. When they make a takeout double with minimum opening bid values and a doubleton in an unbid major suit, and then when they correct to what they believe to be a better contract, both the doubler and his partner know what is going on. However, their opponents read a totally different significance into the auction and call the Director for assistance when the misleading auction causes them to go wrong.

Mind you, when International Teams played against the Italians, they were informed in advance of the strange nature of what the Blue Team used in the guise of takeout doubles, so no opponent could claim injury when non-standard auctions were generated. The problem that occurs today is because of unawareness on the part of the opponents of those who unwittingly use these non-standard doubles for takeout today in the competitive arena. Of course, these methods are permissable, but those who use them are usually unaware that they have an obligation to alert their opponents to the non-standard usage. This is simply because they do not know that their usage is non-standard.

TAKEOUT DOUBLES — TYPE IV

The newest entry into the takeout double arena is a takeout double which, when heard, might be Type I or Type II. When either of these types is the cause of the takeout double, the usage is standard and no alert is required. Type III requires an alert, since it is so decidedly out of the realm of what is standard. Today's expert may also make a Type IV takeout double which, although it does not require an early alert, may require an alert at the time of the rebid by the takeout doubler.

The Type IV takeout double is one that can be made, by agreement, with support for only two of the three unbid suits. The doubler will hold the two higher ranking of the three suits which have not yet been bid. The Type IV double requires that the pair include in its agreements the principle of EQUAL LEVEL CORRECTION.

When the opening bid is one spade, the takeout double guarantees support for hearts and diamonds (unless it is Type II), but may have minimum values and no support for the lowest ranking suit, clubs. When the opening bid is one heart, the takeout double shows support for spades and diamonds, but again may lack support for clubs. When the opening bid is in a minor suit, the takeout double will include both major suits, but may not include the other minor.

The takeout doubler may hold an uneven hand with a four card major suit and five or six diamonds when he doubles an opening bid in the other major suit. He may also hold five-five in the major suits when he makes a takeout double of either minor suit. In all cases, because he did not make a Top and Bottom Cue Bid, he will have length in the two Top suits, excluding the suit of the opening bid, and may have no support at all for the lowest of the three suits normally expected by the takeout double. Holding a hand with five-five in the major suits in the range of six to eleven high card points (assuming the presence of two defensive tricks), a takeout double of a minor suit opening bid will serve to more than adequately describe the hand which once required a Michaels Cue Bid.

Let us digress to say that when an opponent has opened in a minor suit and you hold a major suit five-five hand which is better than the typical Michaels hand, your hand will be good enough to overcall in spades and plan to bid hearts at your next turn. A five-five hand in the strength range to have been described by the use of Michaels will not be good enough to be shown by overcalling in spades and bidding hearts later. So, we see an easy road to describing the hand which once used the precious Cue Bid of the opponents' suit. Since we can double holding only the top two suits when a minor suit is opened by the opponents, we observe clearly that Michaels is no longer needed.

The reason that it is possible to make a Type IV takeout double promising only that the doubler holds the two higher ranking suits, is because the partnership has agreed to incorporate the principal of Equal Level Correction. When you have made a Type IV takeout double and the Advancer (your partner) has bid the lowest ranking of the three remaining suits for which you have no support, you are permitted to correct to the lower ranking of the two remaining suits without showing any extra values.

When you make the call which indicates to your partner that you do not have extra values, but do hold just the two top suits for your takeout double, it will sound to the opponents as though you are expressing a Type II. Since your partner knows that the opponents might be misled at this point in the auction, he must alert. If asked, he must express that he knows from this auction that your takeout double is based on holdings in the two top suits without support for the lowest ranking suit in which you have responded, and that you do not have the extra values usually shown by this kind of auction.

When the auction is: 1♥ - Double - Pass - 2♣, Pass - 2♦, you promise that you hold diamonds and spades, but you do not promise the extra values of a Type II takeout double. When the auction is: 1♦ - Double - Pass - 2♣, Pass - 2♥, you promise major suits, but no extra values. In this auction you may have a typical Michaels hand of five-five in the major suits and six to eleven high card points. When the auction is: 1♠ - Double - Pass - 2♣, Pass - 2♦, you promise diamonds and hearts, but again do not promise any extra values.

Notice that in all of these cases, your takeout double is based on holding the top two unbid suits. In each instance, if your partner, the Advancer, responds to the takeout double by bidding in the lowest ranking of the three remaining suits, when you correct as cheaply as possible to the lower ranking of the two remaining suits, you indicate that your takeout double has no support for the lowest ranking suit.

The correction is not always made from the club suit. Another auction to consider is one which begins with an opening bid of one club. After a takeout double, the Advancer bids diamonds. When the doubler next corrects to hearts without increasing the level, he again shows that his takeout double was based on both major suits, and that there was no support for the unbid minor suit in the hand of the takeout doubler.

Having adopted the principal of Equal Level Correction into the partnership, we should consider how the auction might proceed when the takeout doubler has a Type II hand. He has doubled rather than overcalled due to the strength of his hand and his excellent self sufficient suit. When that suit is the suit which he would need to bid in an auction of Equal Level Correction in order to show his Type II takeout double, he must jump rather than bid his suit cheaply.

Consider the difference between these two auctions:

1) 1♥ - Double - Pass - 2♣, Pass - 2♦ . . . . . and

2) 1♥ - Double - Pass - 2♣, Pass - 3♦

The first of these two auctions shows Equal Level Correction. It indicates that the double was Type IV, based on diamonds and spades and not showing any extra values. In the second auction, the takeout doubler has shown a Type II takeout double, with an excellent diamond suit and about seventeen high card points. However, when the Type II takeout doubler holds a suit which is not the suit in which Equal Level Correction would be made, he does not need to jump to paint a correct picture of his hand. Consider these auctions:

1) 1♣ - Double - Pass - 1♦, Pass - 1♠ . . . . . . or

2) 1♦ - Double - Pass - 2♣, Pass - 2♠

Since the doubler did not bid in the suit in which Equal Level Correction would have been made, instead of an Equal Level Correction message of no extra values, the doubler has promised a Type II hand with an excellent suit and substantial values.

1) 1♦ - Double - Pass - 2♣, Pass - 2♥ . . . . is Equal Level Correction, but

2) 1♦ - Double - Pass - 2♣, Pass - 3♥ shows a Type II takeout double with excellent values and a fine heart suit.

If all of this is a bit confusing, go back and read it again (or several more times) to make sure that you understand the difference between the expression of extra values by the takeout doubler (showing a Type II takeout double) and a rebid by the takeout doubler which expresses Equal Level Correction (which does not imply any values beyond those suggested by the original takeout double).

Another thing to note is that a takeout double was chosen rather than an overcall. When the intruder holds a good major suit and diamonds, it is clear that rather than try to show both suits by making a Type IV takeout double which shows the unbid major suit and diamonds, he will instead overcall in his good major suit. The logical conclusion in auctions when Equal Level Correction shows diamonds and a major suit is that the major suit is either not long enough or strong enough to have been shown by an overcall. The use of the Type IV takeout double and Equal Level Correction strongly implies that diamonds are likely to be longer and/or stronger than the major suit indicated.

When the Equal Level Correction auction shows both majors, there is no such implication. The only inference that can be drawn is that the takeout doubler's hand was not good enough to overcall spades, then bid hearts when five-five, or that the majors are unequal in length with a good four card suit and a mediocre five card suit.

After all of this exposition, it is time for us to examine some example hands:

♠ KJ85
♥ QJ103
♦ 7
♣ AJ87

When the opening bid is one diamond and you are next to call, you have a classic takeout double. You have four card support for each of the unbid suits and roughly the values of an opening bid. When partner selects one of the suits you have shown by making your takeout double, you will not bid again unless partner makes a forcing call.

♠ K5
♥ AQ65
♦ K854
♣ J108

When the opening bid is one spade, you again have a very reasonable takeout double. When the opening bid is one club and your partnership agreement is to double to show that you have an opening hand, your partner must alert every such double. It is not correct to refer to this as a takeout double — it is really a value-showing double rather than a hand that can support any suit partner might bid. If you do double and partner bids spades, what do you do next? If by agreement you can next bid one notrump, that call must also be alerted, since in standard bidding when you double one club and remove partner's call of one spade to one notrump, you have shown a balanced hand too good for an overcall of one notrump. Your value range should be nineteen or twenty points in high cards.

♠ AQ8
♥ KQ965
♦ 74
♣ K62

When the opening bid is one club, with this hand you would clearly overcall by bidding one heart. If you were to make a takeout double, then correct to hearts if your partner responds in diamonds, your partner would believe that spades were as viable as hearts, and might correct to spades holding three spades and two hearts. When the opening bid is one diamond, there are those who would make a takeout double since they hold support for all of the unbid suits. Although this approach has a following in the expert community, there is a true problem attached to the use of a takeout double with this hand, or with any hand which includes five cards in one major and only three cards in the other.

The Advancer will often hold four cards in one major and three cards in the other major when he hears a takeout double. In such instances, he will clearly opt to respond in his four card major suit, rather than even consider bidding in the three card holding. When your takeout double includes five cards in one major and three in the other, it is probable that partner will bid his four card major which fits with your three card holding, and the five-three fit in the other major will not be found. For this reason, we recommend that when holding five-three in the major suits, it is correct not to make a takeout double, but rather to overcall in the five card suit. This will make it possible to name the five-three fit as trumps rather than to play in the four-three fit.

♠ AJ98
♥ 7
♦ KJ10864
♣ A3

When the opening bid has been one club and you hold this hand, if you are still playing Michaels Cue Bids you are out of luck. You have to overcall one diamond and run the risk of losing the spade suit. When you have graduated to Top and Bottom Cue Bids, your bid of two clubs describes this hand to a tee. What if the opening bid was one heart?

Here is a classic hand for the Type IV takeout double. When you make a takeout double of the one heart opening bid, if partner responds in spades (or diamonds) all is well. If partner responds in clubs, you will make an Equal Level Correction to diamonds. Partner will alert, and if asked, explain that this auction does not show any extra values, but shows only spades and diamonds, with diamonds probably longer or stronger (or both) than spades.

♠ KJ1085
♥ AQ873
♦ 94
♣ 6

This is a typical maximum for the use of the Michaels Cue Bid. Now that we don't have that tool, we make a type IV takeout double if the opening bid is in either minor suit. If the Advancer responds in the unbid minor suit, we correct to hearts, giving partner a choice of major suits. Of course, he alerts when we bid hearts and when asked, he explains that the auction has shown both major suits, no support for the minor suit in which he has responded, and minimum values for a competitive action.

♠ KQ94
♥ J8742
♦ AQ3
♣ 8

When the opening bid is one club, a takeout double (Type I) is easy. When the opening bid is one diamond, you can still make a takeout double. If the Advancer bids two clubs, you can correct to two hearts to deny interest in clubs, show both majors, and also deny any values beyond the minimum for a takeout double.

♠ A6
♥ AKJ1064
♦ AJ9
♣ 107

After an opening bid in either minor suit, we need to show this powerful hand with its excellent suit. An overcall would not be adequate, since we need to find very little in values in the Advancer's hand in order to make a game. So, we make a Type II takeout double. When partner responds to the double by bidding two spades, our next call of three hearts will identify this type of hand.

When Advancer bids two of the unbid minor suit, however, in order to show this hand we cannot simply bid two hearts. A call of two hearts would be Equal Level Correction, showing minimum takeout double values and both major suits (Type IV). To show this hand with its Type II takeout double, we should next jump to three hearts.

♠ AQ4
♥ KQ9
♦ QJ106
♣ AJ8

After an opening bid in any suit, we would like to make an overcall in notrump to show this powerful balanced hand. However, an overcall of one notrump by agreement usually shows fifteen to seventeen (or 14 to 17, or 15 to 18) high card points. This hand is clearly too good for that action.

An overcall of two notrump shows a completely different kind of hand. It should be the Unusual Notrump, showing both minor suits with at least five-five distribution and specific value ranges (see Part II of this book).

We show this excellent balanced hand by making a takeout double, and then bidding notrump at our next turn to call. An auction generated in this fashion indicates a powerful balanced hand, too good for an immediate overcall of one notrump. This, again, is a Type II takeout double.

♠ K5
♥ Q1074
♦ KJ73
♣ A62

The theme of our second example returns. When the opening bid is one spade, a takeout double (Type I) is reasonable. When the opening bid is in any other suit, the recommended call is pass. In this age of paper thin competitive bidding, that may sound like heresy. However, the aggressive competitive bidder who is successful understands that his success depends upon animated competition with distributional hands, not balanced hands that just happen to include thirteen high card points.

CHAPTER V
OVERCALLING WITH FOUR CARD SUITS

In researching the subject of this chapter, we opened and read from the classic source of information, The *Complete Book on Overcalls in Contract Bridge,* by Mike Lawrence.

In 1979, this writer had the privilege to be the editor and publisher of Mike's exceptional book on the subject of overcalls. Having reread the short presentation on the topic to be covered in this chapter, we asked Mike for permission to quote the pages in that book which cover the topic. He graciously gave that permission. So, here is what Mike Lawrence had to say about four card suit overcalls in 1979.

* *

Overcalling on Four Card Suits

Every now and then, you are going to find yourself with some sort of goodish hand and your RHO opens the bidding. Feeling like you should take some action, but finding nothing convenient, you pass and later discover you had some game or partial available on a hand where neither you nor partner had been able to enter the auction. Certainly there are hands with which you would open the bidding but with which you can't compete after an opening bid. Some of these hands, however, can be handled through the tactic of overcalling on a four card suit. There are many cases where this is correct but there are not many generalities available. So, instead, the usual examples.

With no one vul., RHO opens 1♦ :

1♦: ♠ KQ109
    ♥ 42
    ♦ AQ65
    ♣ K54

Bid one spade. One of the few generalities I can give is that overcalling on a four card suit requires a very good suit. Partner is going to raise whenever possible and three small should be quite adequate support if his hand is otherwise suited. Responder should not have to be worried about the quality of your overcalls.

1♦: ♠ 82
    ♥ AQ107
    ♦ 107654
    ♣ AQ

One heart. If the possession of five cards in the suit opened bothers you, forget it. Your length in diamonds plus opener's length assures you that your partner (and LHO) are also short. This means your partner is likely to have heart support. The length in diamonds therefore is not a minus but, rather, an asset. Perhaps the two hands are something like this:

        ♠ A9764
        ♥ J83
        ♦ 3
        ♣ 7652

        ♠ 82
        ♥ AQ107
        ♦ 107654
        ♣ AQ

With a diamond lead and a heart return, you should make between seven and nine tricks. Not bad considering that dummy is not all that good. If dummy had a fourth heart, ten tricks would be possible and if you found dummy with five of them, game would depend on winning either the club or heart finesse. With the opening bid on your right, game should be nearly a cinch.

Now, if game is on opposite:

♠ A842
♥ J954
♦ 3
♣ J942

it would be nice to bid it. Or, if you can't get to game, at least get to hearts. Making 170 is better than being -110 or -90 or some such part score. If you don't bid 1♥ right away you will never be able to reach four hearts or, for that matter, hearts, period.

1♦: ♠ KQJ9
    ♥ A2
    ♦ 43
    ♣ J8743

One spade. This hand may appear similar to the prior hand, but it is, in fact, quite different. There is a rather subtle difference. The points are the same. The distribution is the same. The hand contains a good four card suit and a crummy five card suit. Neither hand contains a singleton.

The difference? It is in the auction. In the previous hand the opening bid was in your weak five card suit. This had the effect of implying that your partner would have substantial distributional support for your four card suit. Even if you found partner with no high cards at all, you were assured of some kind of fit.

In this hand, however, the opening bid was in one of your doubletons. Therefore, even though it's correct to bid one spade, you do so in the hope, rather than the expectation, that partner can provide some sort of fit. If worst comes to worst, you will probably take three spade tricks and the ace of hearts. But my estimation of this hand is that you will seldom get less than five tricks, even opposite nothing. There are many hands with five card suits on which nearly everyone would overcall which could easily end up taking fewer tricks.

1♦: ♠ AQ862
♥ AQ3
♦ 42
♣ 973

This hand, if doubled in a one spade overcall could conceivably take only two tricks. While two tricks is, admittedly, unlikely, the possibility of taking three or four is very real. And yet, nearly everyone would hasten to bid one spade on this hand, and hasten equally to pass the hand just being discussed with KQJ9 of spades. My own feeling is such that I would be quite pleased to hold

♠ KQJ9
♥ A2
♦ 43
♣ J8743

and be able to overcall one spade at matchpoints, rubber bridge, IMP's, or, for that matter, board-a-match.

There is another aspect of this hand which is important to recognize. If you elect to overcall one spade, you have to be prepared to lose the club suit. There is no way you can ever hope to get the club suit mentioned without partner assuming (rightly) that you have as many or more spades than clubs.

Hands like these are inflexible. Either you don't bid at all, or you bid (as in the example) one spade and then forever subside. It is true that you may bid again. You may accept a game try if you have a maximum, or if partner bids notrump, there are hands on which you could raise. Perhaps, once in a while, your partner will bid your five card suit and then you can raise. But, for the most part, once you've overcalled, you will take no more voluntary action and will essentially leave it up to partner.

There are conventions which you might be using: Michaels,

Hi-Lo cue bids, Astro cue bids, etc. If it suits you, you might use one of these if you happen to be using the right one at the right time. But, if not, then consider the overcall. Far better to describe some of your hand than none at all.

You may wonder why overcalling on four card suits is so effective. Aside from the usual reasons, a four card suit overcall needs a good suit by definition, so it is certainly a suit you want partner to lead. The fact that you have such a good suit suggests partner would not have much in the way of high cards in the suit and it might not occur to him to lead it without a suggestion from you. Furthermore, the quality of your suit is such that the opponents may be shy about contracting for some number of notrump. They may credit you for a longer suit and decide on a part-score when three notrump is cold.

Having only a four bagger works out additionally in that when partner leads it, you may find yourself taking two or three tricks in the suit against a suit contract. Each opponent, holding three or even four small may have been hoping his partner held shortness in the suit. When this happens, you will occasionally find the opponents getting too high in the wrong suit. It's not bad when your opponents miss a game; but when you can get them into the wrong game and then beat it when another game (usually 3NT) is cold, it's even better.

By now, if you've not been convinced that overcalling on four card suits is a good thing for your side if done properly, do this: first, review the two hands at the introduction of this chapter. Then, during the next session or two you play, note the ease or difficulty you experience when your opponents overcall.

If you are convinced it's right to compete, then consider this: it is a fact that people do not compete with four baggers. If a partnership which did not tend to do this decided it was right, then they would be in a position to compete on from one to three or four hands more per session than they had been in the past. My experience suggests that, in general, my matchpoint results are excellent where one of these overcalls has been used. Out of ten occurrences, I would expect two or three tops, four very good results, a average or two, and, perhaps, one bad result. At IMP's bad results just don't happen. The reason is that the worst thing that happens is a small plus like 70 or 90 instead of 110 or 130. At IMP's you just don't worry about small differentials.

So, if you give these a try, you will be well placed. At least until everyone else learns as well. I do understand that if you are not accustomed to something like this, it is difficult to make the transition. I hope you don't make it against me.

Some more examples in the same vein. This time you are not vul. vs. vul. and your RHO opens one heart.

1♥: ♠ KQ108
    ♥ 32
    ♦ AJ43
    ♣ K65

Don't get carried away. This is a takeout double, not a one spade overcall.

1♥: ♠ A2
    ♥ 108654
    ♦ A2
    ♣ KQJ8

Pass. Overcalling at the two level requires a five card suit. Two clubs, good suit and all, is just a bit rich.

1♥: ♠ K1097
    ♥ A9542
    ♦ 42
    ♣ K3

This is the kind of hand on which a theoretically unsound bid of one spade could work well. It's the sort of "bad" bid you can get away with at matchpoints, but definitely not IMP's. Bear in mind that you are trading heavily on the fact that you expect to find a fit because of your heart length.

Even though you don't take much room away from the opponents by your one spade overall, look what might happen. Compare these three auctions:

1.) 1♥   Pass   1NT   Pass
     2♣   ?

2.) 1♥   Pass   1NT   Pass
     Pass   ?

3.) 1♥   1♠   Pass   2♠
     ?

In auction one, the opponents have been able to find their best fit (probably) and whether or not your side balances, they can judge what to do over your belated competition.

Likewise, in auction two. If you bid 2♠ now it is somewhat dangerous, although probably correct.

In auction three, however, you have kept the opponents from their smooth exchange, and at the same time you got to two because your partner likes spades which on auction two was not so clear.

1♥: ♠ AKQ9
     ♥ 872
     ♦ Q43
     ♣ 1097

After a heart opening you should get in there with one spade at matchpoints, but only at matchpoints. You would have preferred the opening bid to be one club instead of one heart because you would have deprived the opponents of far more bidding room.

1♥: ♠ QJ42
     ♥ 87653
     ♦ K10
     ♣ K2

Again, at matchpoints, one spade should be both safe and effective. The reason you shouldn't try this at IMP's is that you could go for a large number. At matchpoints, this is not serious if you score some victories, however small, but IMP scoring requires some degree of caution, and cautious one spade is not.

1♥: ♠ Q987
    ♥ 87642
    ♦ K10
    ♣ K2

This shows you the degree to which you might stretch things. At matchpoints, one spade is not as silly as it may seem. It's a bad bid, but you may well get away with it. Remember that you would never try this unless you had some reason to expect a fit, i.e. your heart length.

1♥: ♠ QJ97
    ♥ 86542
    ♦ A
    ♣ AJ10

With this one you are getting close to a minimum one spade call at IMP's At matchpoints, for sure. At IMP's this is reasonably safe. You have four or more likely tricks and you may score an incredible game now and then. Give partner

♠ K8642
♥ J
♦ 10863
♣ Q93

and four spades is possible. And you will be able to grab quite a few part-score swings.

♠ 10863
♥ Q2
♦ KQ63
♣ 964

With this dummy, you can likely make two or, on a good day, three spades. At the same time they can make three diamonds in spite of your impressive trump holding.

1♥: ♠ KJ87
    ♥ 42
    ♦ AK
    ♣ Q6432

Pass is probably best. With no reason to expect a fit, it is too dangerous to attempt any action. If you must bid something, I suppose one spade is best, but I don't care for it. Be sure you understand why this hand is a pass when it is actually better than the last three examples.

1♥: ♠ KQ105
    ♥ 8642
    ♦ AJ3
    ♣ 76

One spade is reasonable at matchpoints Holding four hearts is not as great an inducement for you to bid as holding five hearts would be, but they do suggest a fit is possible. Don't try this one at IMP's.

1♥: ♠ KQJ3
    ♥ 876
    ♦ AJ4
    ♣ KJ5

This is probably a better double than it is a spade bid. If partner has four spades, he will bid them. If not, the odds favor his holding a five card minor. At matchpoints or at IMP's, this hand is too good to pass. Try double.

* *

Mike has expanded on this short presentation in his "Topics on Bridge" series. For more information on overcalling with four card suits, try that source.*

The important points that Mike has made about overcalling with four card suits are these:

1. The suit must be a very good suit.
2. The four card overcall should only be made at the one level.
3. The longer your holding in the suit bid in front of you, the greater your safety factor becomes, since partner is more likely to have a fit for your four card suit.

In Mike's example in which the overcall was made on four good spades after an opening bid in a suit in which a doubleton was held. He presented a hand which had the advantage of a second suit, a poor five card minor suit. He makes the point that other tools may permit the bidder to show both suits, negating the necessity to overcall and put all of the bidder's eggs in one basket. That point fits in exactly with the concept that this book has set out to present. We would have used a Top & Bottom Cue Bid holding four spades and five clubs, rather than need to use the four card overcall at the risk of losing the club suit.

On the third hand from the end where Mike suggests a pass, those of us who have adopted Top & Bottom Cue Bids would surely use that tool. We agree with Mike that the overcall of one spade with that hand would not be a very good action. But, with the ability to show two suits, it is fairly clear to use Top & Bottom to show both spades and clubs, with longer clubs.

Nearly two decades have passed, but Mike's observations on overcalling with four card suits remain as valid now as when he first presented them.

*See page 159 to order "Topics on Bridge" and "Overcalls" by Lawrence.

CHAPTER SIX
ORGANIZING OUR TOOLS AND SOLVING THE PROBLEMS

In the previous five chapters we first posed a bidding problem which, until now, few players believed was worthy of being solved by conventional means; then we introduced tools which can be used to solve that problem.

Let us summarize the methods we have presented.

1. TOP AND BOTTOM CUE BIDS. This conventional approach addresses the problem of bidding hands with a longer or stronger (or both) minor suit, as well as a shorter or weaker (or both) major suit. These are hands which appear often and for which there has been no language to express.

Use of a cue bid of the suit opened by the opponents has been routinely been assigned to show two suits of five cards or more (usually equal in length) with emphasis on majors. The prevailing mood has been that the Michaels Cue Bid is a panacea, and little thought has been given to putting the cue bid to better use.

We believe that for best use, the cue bid should be assigned the meaning that the bidder has the highest and lowest ranking unbid suits, usually with greater length or strength (or both) in the lower suit. With some variations which enhance the structure, the use of Michaels should be replaced with this particular tool.

2. CONVENTIONAL JUMP OVERCALLS. When the shorter or weaker major suit is hearts, the Top and Bottom Cue Bid will not always be an available description. When the bidder holds hearts and a minor suit, and when the opening bid is in the other minor suit, the Cue Bid does not show those two specific suits, so some other method should be available which does show those suits. For this purpose, we suggest a jump overcall in the other minor suit after an opposing minor suit has been bid. Using this convention, the bidder not only holds the minor suit he has bid, but a shorter or weaker holding in the heart suit as well.

3. TYPE 4 TAKEOUT DOUBLES. There remains a necessity to be able to bid those hands which contain the two higher ranking of the three remaining suits after an opposing opening bid. To describe those hands, we adopt a new approach to takeout doubles.

Most doubles for takeout will either contain support for all three of the unbid suits or will later show a hand that was too good for an overcall. However, when the takeout doubler hears the Advancer bid in the lowest of the three unbid suits in response to a takeout double, when he holds only the two higher ranking suits, the takeout doubler applies the principle of EQUAL LEVEL CORRECTION. When he corrects from the lowest ranking suit which has been bid by the Advancer to the lower ranking of the two remaining suits, he indicates that his takeout double was based only upon support for the two higher ranking suits, but does not show any extra values beyond the minimum expected for a normal takeout double.

Correction to the lower ranking of the two remaining suits shows only minimum competitive values. When the doubler does hold a hand which was too good for an overcall, if his suit is the lower of the two remaining suits in such an auction, he must jump in his suit to describe his excellent suit and extra values.

4. FOUR CARD SUIT OVERCALLS. When the opening bidder has started by naming the intruder's longer suit, if his shorter suit is a good suit and he is able to mention it at the one level, his overcall in a four card suit has great merit. The Advancer will nearly always be short in the suit which was named by the opening bid and long in the overcaller's hand, and the Advancer will usually hold a fit for the suit of the overcall.

He will not know that the suit is only four cards in length, but he will know that his fit for the suit of the overcall, shortness in opener's suit, and moderate values are enough to support the overcall in most instances.

Let us keep these tools firmly in mind, and now set out to solve the thirty problems which were posed in Chapter One. Here goes...

1.   ♠ J943
     ♥ J98
     ♦ 4
     ♣ AK854

Proposing to take action with this minimum hand can be dangerous. The values are meager, although the shape is reasonably good. When the opening bid is one diamond, this hand falls short of the requisites for a takeout double. An overcall of two clubs has some appeal since it takes the one level away from the responder. The club suit, however, is not all that imposing. If the Advancer does not fit with clubs, an overcall might lead to a substantial penalty. However, the chances of finding a fit in either clubs or spades increases the possibility of a reasonable scenario. At matchpoints, not vulnerable versus vulnerable, you might reasonably create some action by making a Top and Bottom Cue Bid against an opening bid in either red suit.

2.   ♠ —
     ♥ 9865
     ♦ AQJ92
     ♣ KQ98

As was suggested in Chapter One, when the opening bid is one spade you are not ashamed to make a takeout double with this hand. When the opening bid is one club, you would like to show your good diamond suit without shutting out the possibility of playing in hearts if partner has length there. The conventional jump overcall of two diamonds will show both red suits with emphasis on longer or stronger (or both) diamonds than hearts. Could you ask for a more reasonable way to compete and describe this hand?

3. ♠ 73
   ♥ K652
   ♦ Q
   ♣ QJ8643

This hand has a paucity of high cards, but excellent shape. At favorable vulnerability, particularly at match points, you might wish to create some action after an opponent has opened the bidding in either of the pointed suits. When the opening bid is one spade, a cue bid of two spades will show clubs and hearts with longer or stronger (or both) clubs. When the opening bid is one diamond, a jump to three clubs again shows your suits and emphasis on clubs.

4. ♠ AQ108
   ♥ A102
   ♦ J
   ♣ AK1063

It is always nice to deal with a hand which not only has good shape, but also good values. Here, against an opening bid of one diamond you can make a takeout double since you have reasonable support for all of the unbid suits along with your good values. When the opening bid is one heart, a cue bid of two hearts will show the black suits with an emphasis on clubs. When the opening bid is one club, you might try an overcall in your good four card spade suit.

5. ♠ K1043
   ♥ 3
   ♦ 54
   ♣ AJ9632

Here we reach a normal minimum (if not vulnerable) for a Top and Bottom Cue Bid bid when an opponent opens with either red suit. We are not ashamed of our holdings in either clubs or spades after the description that our cue bid will carry to partner. When the opening bid is one club, the spade suit is not good enough to consider an overcall.

6. ♠ K983
    ♥ A53
    ♦ KJ10652
    ♣ —

When the opening bid is one club, a slightly off shape takeout double is not unreasonable. When the opening bid is one heart, you should wish to show diamonds and spades. You can make a takeout double, and if the Advancer responds by bidding two clubs, you can correct to two diamonds. This will show that you have no support for clubs, but will not suggest any more than minimum values for your takeout double. Since you did not overcall in spades, you also suggest that your diamonds are more imposing than your spades.

7. ♠ KJ
    ♥ A1064
    ♦ AKQ93
    ♣ 54

How nice again to hold good values. When the opening bid is one club, you have an easy jump overcall of two diamonds to show your red suit holdings. If the Advancer bids two hearts, you are good enough to raise to three hearts, even if vulnerable; if he jumps to three hearts, you will be happy to bid a game. When the opening bid is one spade you can make a takeout double, and if the Advancer responds in clubs, you can correct to diamonds to give him a choice of suits. Since his response in clubs denies length in either red suit, you need not push forward with your good values. When the opening bid is one diamond, your heart suit is suspect for a four card overcall, but your values are so good that you should probably go ahead and make that call, or you might overcall one notrump.

8.   ♠ J9742
     ♥ 2
     ♦ 94
     ♣ KQ985

Back to bad values but excellent shape. Against a red suit opening bid (if not vulnerable) you might try a Top and Bottom Cue Bid. Don't even dream of overcalling in spades when they open with one club.

9.   ♠ Q
     ♥ 98652
     ♦ A9
     ♣ AKJ107

Here is a hand completely designed for our tools. Without them, how could you possibly compete with confidence against an opening bid in either spades or diamonds? The Top and Bottom Cue Bid when they open with one spade, or the jump overcall of three clubs when the opening bid is one diamond, are wonderful tools to employ with this hand.

10.   ♠ 8
     ♥ AKQ4
     ♦ 1094
     ♣ AQ432

This hand with its good values and shape is easy to bid versus an opening bid in any suit. When they open with one heart, overcall in clubs. When they open with one club, overcall one heart. When they open with one diamond, jump to three clubs to show your suit lengths and values. When they open with one spade, you have your choice of either a Top and Bottom Cue Bid or a takeout double (how well do you like your diamonds?).

11. ♠ AJ42
    ♥ 42
    ♦ AJ865
    ♣ A4

When they open with one spade, you should overcall two diamonds. When they open with one diamond, an overcall of one spade would overstate your suit quality, but not a lot. When they open with one club, a Top and Bottom Cue Bid is in order. When they open with one heart, you can make a takeout double and correct to diamonds if the Advancer responds by bidding two clubs.

12. ♠ K743
    ♥ AQ
    ♦ AKJ106
    ♣ J5

When the opening bid is one heart, make a takeout double and correct to diamonds if the Advancer bids clubs. If the opening bid is one club, you have a classic Top and Bottom Cue Bid. When the opening bid is one spade, a two diamond overcall is easy. When the opening bid is one diamond, your spade suit is not nearly good enough for a four card overcall, but you can double. Then convert any suit response to notrump to show a hand too good for an immediate overcall of one notrump.

13. ♠ KQ86
    ♥ 9
    ♦ Q43
    ♣ AK1094

Against an opening bid in either red suit, you can cue bid. When they open the bidding in either black suit, you can overcall in the other. If you like your diamond holding, you can make a takeout double instead of emphasizing the black suits by cue bidding when the opening bid has been one heart.

14. ♠ 103
    ♥ K864
    ♦ J8
    ♣ KQJ105

When they open with one heart, you will overcall two clubs. When the opening bid is one club, forget the heart overcall on this bad suit. When they open with one spade, you can cue bid. When they open with one diamond, you can jump to three clubs.

15. ♠ Q93
    ♥ AQ86
    ♦ 3
    ♣ AQ873

Against an opening bid of one diamond, a takeout double is fine. When the opening bid is one spade, a cue bid will show your clubs and hearts. When they open with either one club or one heart, you can overcall in the other of those two suits.

16. ♠ 752
    ♥ KQ82
    ♦ 4
    ♣ AK1093

Rather than make a takeout double of an opening bid of one diamond, since our spades are so poor we prefer the jump to three clubs. When the opening bid is one spade, we make a cue bid. When the opening bid is in either clubs or hearts, we overcall in the other of those suits.

17. ♠ 74
    ♥ AQJ7
    ♦ 54
    ♣ A10852

A cue bid is our choice when they open with one spade. A

jump to three clubs is also our choice after an opening bid of one diamond. When the opening bid is one club, we like an overcall of one heart. When the opening bid is one heart, we prefer pass. We would like a better club suit to overcall at the two level, particularly if vulnerable. If at match points and not vulnerable, well . . .

18. ♠ AQ954
♥ 3
♦ 10
♣ AKQ1082

It is clear here to overcall in the other black suit when they open the bidding in either spades or clubs. When standard methods are in use, an overcall in clubs is the classic action after a red suit opening bid, with the bidder planning to rebid spades, even at a high level, at his next turn.

But what if there is no next turn? We make a Top and Bottom Cue Bid after an opening bid in either red suit knowing that partner will certainly give us another turn to bid. If he retreats to clubs, as he will be expected to do since he probably has very limited values, we now freely bid spades. This indicates a powerful hand with at least five-five distribution in the two suits that have been shown, urges partner to bid a game with almost nothing, and consider a slam with any working cards.

19. ♠ AQ102
♥ 3
♦ Q9863
♣ KQ9

Against an opening bid of one heart, a standard takeout double is perfect. When the opening bid is one club, we make a cue bid. When the opening bid is one diamond, a one spade overcall is fine. But when the opening bid is one spade, we go quietly — the diamond suit is just too poor for a two level overcall.

20. ♠ AJ82
    ♥ A83
    ♦ Q
    ♣ AJ985

A takeout double of one diamond is fine. When they open with one heart, make a Top and Bottom Cue Bid. When they open with either one spade or one club, an overcall in the other black suit is reasonable, but a better suit would be preferred in either case.

21. ♠ 4
    ♥ A1094
    ♦ Q10
    ♣ AJ10632

By now it should be getting easy. When they open with one spade, you will cue bid. When they open with one diamond, bid three clubs. When they open with one heart, overcall two clubs. When they open with one club, your heart suit is not quite up to expectancy for a four card suit overcall.

22. ♠ Q8652
    ♥ AK
    ♦ 4
    ♣ AJ865

It would be far nicer to have the bulk of our values in our long suits rather than as a mighty doubleton. Still, a Top and Bottom call after an opening bid in either red suit is fine. A one spade overcall when they open with one club is all right since you do have a five card suit. We would like a better club suit for a two level overcall when they open with one spade, but would probably make that call even though we are not proud of the suit.

23. ♠ AK105
   ♥ —
   ♦ A832
   ♣ AK1043

If these examples seem too good to be true, remember that they were not created to prove our selected methods. They were part of the real hands at a Regional tournament over the span of five sessions.

With this powerhouse we would make a takeout double of a one heart opening bid. When the opening bid is one diamond, we would cue bid and then raise the suit in which partner elected to respond. When the opening bid is one club, we would easily overcall one spade. And, when the opening bid is one spade, we would not only overcall in clubs, but we would also plan to bid notrump at a later turn to give partner a chance to show a fit for our diamond suit (more about this use of Unusual Notrump in Part II).

24. ♠ K7
   ♥ AK98
   ♦ 53
   ♣ QJ652

Again we would cue bid after an opening bid of one spade. We would jump to three clubs after an opening bid of one diamond. We would overcall one heart after an opening bid of one club. However, we would decline to overcall two clubs after an opening bid of one heart on a suit of this quality.

25. ♠ QJ73
   ♥ 7
   ♦ Q76
   ♣ AKJ106

Against an opening bid of one heart, we would make a takeout double. When the opening bid is one diamond, we are happy to cue bid. When the opening bid is one spade, an overcall of two clubs is fine. When the opening bid is one club, the spade suit is not really as good as we would like for an overcall. Still, at matchpoints if the vulnerability is right, we just might overcall anyway.

26. ♠ Q
♥ QJ64
♦ A6
♣ A108743

By now you should be making the right calls on each of these hands against any projected opening bid. Here, against one spade we cue bid. Against one diamond, we jump to three clubs. Against one heart, we will overcall because of the sixth club. Against an opening bid of one club, see the comments in number 25 above.

27. ♠ Q8652
♥ A5
♦ Q
♣ AK654

Make a cue bid after an opening bid in either red suit. Overcall in the other black suit after an opening bid of one spade or one club.

28. ♠ AQ62
♥ 10
♦ 862
♣ KQ973

Do as in number 27 above. The four card suit is pretty good, and the nine of clubs helps that suit.

29.　♠ 75
　　♥ Q983
　　♦ AJ
　　♣ A10542

Back to bad values with our good shape. And poor suits as well. But again at match points, you will want to cue bid after an opening bid of one spade, or jump to three clubs when the opening bid is one diamond, particularly when the vulnerability is right. Forget about overcalling in either clubs or hearts when they open with the other one of those two suits.

30.　♠ A6532
　　♥ K
　　♦ KJ9875
　　♣ 6

Saving the freak for last!! Because of the extra shape we would take any of the four actions against any of the four opening bids. Cue bid against an opening bid of one club. When the opening bid is one heart, double and correct from clubs to diamonds, if necessary. Bid one spade over one diamond, or two diamonds over one spade.

Back in Chapter One, you probably didn't dream that the problems presented could be solved so easily. For most of the world out there, they cannot. We do not understand why the creation of methods to bid these hands did not happen years ago, and that is exactly why this book has been written. The author and his regular partners have been using these methods for more than a decade.

We lament not having been on the November Panel of the Master Solvers' Club (most panelists appear every fourth month). We would have taken that opportunity to suggest problem A should not have been solved by random guesses. We wonder how the moderator would have rated our answer at that time?

PART TWO

THE
UNUSUAL NOTRUMP

CHAPTER SEVEN
UNUSUAL OVERCALLS
IN NOTRUMP

Perhaps the most misunderstood and misused tool available to competitive bidders is the Unusual Notrump. We have repeatedly seen instances of its use with the wrong distribution or the wrong values. It is routinely included with the expected bidding tools that are used by virtually everyone who plays the game, but is it truly comprehended? Has it, in fact, been completely defined and codified? Let us see what the standard sources have to say.

The Official Encyclopedia of Bridge, Fifth Edition gives the Unusual Notrump just more than one full page. It gives credit for devising the convention to Alvin Roth who developed it with Tobias Stone. The coverage is reasonably complete. Twelve sample auctions are shown, but only three example hands. Our discussion will cover each of the situations mentioned in this source.

Bridge Conventions Complete, by Amalya Kearse, presents but a capsule of information on the convention. However, in addition to a listing for the Unusual Notrump Overcall and a little more than two short pages of coverage, this reference gets into several variations. There are: Unusual One Notrump Overcall, Unusual Notrump and Minors, and Unusual Notrump and Minors Over Notrump. A Section titled Two-Suited Takeouts — In Profile, is given the job of describing the intent of various cue bids, as well as the topic which we intend to give thorough coverage here.

Bridge Conventions, by Edwin B. Kantar does a more complete job, with eight typewritten pages on the subject, concluded by a quiz. Kantar spends reasonable effort in distinguishing the Unusual Notrump from notrump overcalls and balancing notrumps.

Modern Bridge Conventions, by William S. Root and Richard Pavlicek begins with a good presentation of suit length requirements and value ranges. It follows with a brief presentation on responses, then rebids by the Unusual Notrump bidder. A section called Further Applications follows, then another on the use of four notrump.

Our own thoughts and ideas will expand on the information included in all four sources. Our goal will be to bring into focus just what we believe all players who wish to use the Unusual Notrump properly will need to know.

THE THEORY OF BIDS THAT HAVE OPPOSITE MEANINGS

An interesting phenomon regarding bidding exists. Bids which have a specific meaning can be used in two ways. They can mean what they are supposed to mean, but when used in different contexts which clarify their intent, they will take on a completely opposite meaning than the originally defined one.

For example, one of the official words used in bidding is — "double." The function of using the word "double" in an auction is to increase the penalties for undertricks when the doubler believes that the contracting side is overboard. Of course, not only are the premiums for defeating the contract increased — so are the awards for fulfillment of a contract which has been doubled.

So, within the framework of the scoring system, when a bidder says "double," he is suggesting to his partner that rather than bid on competitively, his side should defend and reap the rewards of increased penalties when the contract established by the opponents fails.

However, does it make sense to double the opponents for penalties early in the auction when they have opened the bidding or responded in a suit against which you have considerable defense? Logically, it does not make sense when the opponents are not yet committed to that choice of trump suit, and left to their own devices will probably bid to a higher level. Perhaps they will select the trump suit for which you have excellent defense at that higher level, and have no place to run after you have made your penalty double.

If it makes no sense for "double" on the first round of bidding to express the desire to increase penalties, then what should it mean? Obviously, you know the answer. Instead of saying, "Partner, do not bid — let us defend and get rich!", double at that stage of the auction says just the opposite. It says, "Partner, rather than defend, I would like to compete. Please bid a suit that you believe might make a good trump suit for our side."

So we see that doubles for penalty and doubles for takeout use the same bidding term to express two totally opposite ideas, and the difference is shown by a predetermined assignment of meaning, based upon the point in the auction at which the word "double" is used.

Another word that may be used during the auction is "notrump." When a bidder uses that word as part of the contract that he suggests his side will fulfill, his message is that there is no good choice for a trump suit, and that a contract at which there literally is no trump suit will be best for the contracting side. This usually means that the contracting side has hands which are relatively balanced, and their prospect for winning tricks with their two balanced hands is mostly from high cards. In short, bids in notrump usually suggest reasonably strong balanced hands.

Al Roth came up with the idea that bids in notrump could also be used to express the exact opposite of the usual meaning. Rather than expressing strong balanced hands, notrump could be used to express weak unbalanced hands. When the message —

1) Which suits are being shown,
2) What the minimum expected lengths might be, and
3) What the value range is expected to be —

could be shown by certain bids in notrump in a competitive auction, a valuable tool could be added to the defensive bidder's arsenal. Thus was born what we today know as the Unusual Notrump.

Through the years of its use, the Unusual Notrump has emerged in several guises. Its most frequest use is that of preemption, but in several auctions it becomes a constructive tool instead. In the pages that follow we will show you the many faces of this interesting and truly useful tool.

SUITS SHOWN BY THE USE OF UNUSUAL NOTRUMP

The suits shown by the use of this convention are either the two minor suits or the two lowest ranking of the three unbid suits. The choice is up to the members of the partnership. When the opening bid is in a major suit, the two minor suits are also the two lower ranking unbid suits, and there is no conflict as to choice of suits.

When the opening bid has been in a minor suit, two schools of thought exist. They are:

1) The two lower of the remaining suits are being shown. This means that when the opening bid has been one club, the Unusual Notrump shows diamonds and hearts, and when the opening bid has been one diamond, the conventional use shows clubs and hearts. This agreement presupposes that the opening minor suit bidder truly has length in the suit of his opening bid, and with that presumption it becomes more reasonable to adapt the call to the two lower of the remaining suits.

2) The minors are still shown by the use of the Unusual Notrump. This agreement comes about since it is known that opening bids in minor suits are frequently made on three card holdings. The bidding side assumes that the opening minor suit will be short often enough so the use of the tool should still offer a choice of minor suits despite the opening bid.

The first of these two choices is the more frequent agreement by tournament players of today, but there are those who believe that using this tool for minor suits, even when the opening bid has been made in a minor, is better.

THE JUMP OVERCALL OF TWO NOTRUMP

The most common use of the Unusual Notrump occurs after an opening bid by the opposing side when the overcaller jumps to two notrump. If some means could be devised to collect just one cent for each misuse of this convention throughout the world and give the proceeds to one designee, the recipient would be so wealthy that he would never again be concerned about money. Although many users do understand the message conveyed by this call, far more either do not have a clear understanding of the meaning of the call, or lack the discipline to wait for the proper hand on which to use it.

The Unusual jump to two notrump should again carry a message of opposites. When used properly, it is either a preemptive bid in two suits or a slam try in two suits. The value range should never be intermediate; even when he holds the expected suit lengths, the Unusual Two Notrump bidder should never have the defensive strength of an opening bid.

When the competitive bidder does have the values of an opening bid, he should bid his hand by overcalling in the higher ranking of the two suits that he wishes to show, and then follow, if possible, by bidding the lower ranking suit at his next turn. He may be unable to impliment this plan due to unusual turns in the auction, but that should be his plan to describe both his suit lengths and his values.

We have observed this same problem in discussing the correct use of the Michaels Cue Bid. The value range for that convention — as written — is that it shows less than an opening bid (some also use it with hands of exceptional strength, which can be shown to be at the opposite end of the value scale in the subsequent auction).

When either the Cue Bid or the Unusual Notrump is used with too much in defensive values, the Advancer will often be misled into taking a "phantom save." That is, he will look at a good fit for one of the suits shown by his partner's action, and not realize that his side has the defensive strength to defeat the opposing contract. So, he will sacrifice against that unmakeable opposing contract. This lack of understanding can lead to very poor results.

Having established that the use of the Unusual Notrump as a jump overcall at the two level is a preemptive bid in two suits, let us also establish that the suit lengths are, minimally, five-five. Again, those who either do not understand or are not disciplined enough to wait for the proper hand for this preemptive action, have often been seen making the call with five-four or six-four distribution. This creates obvious problems.

When the Advancer holds two-two or three-three in the suits shown by the two-suited preemptive bid, he will, as a matter of course, bid the lower ranking of the two. When his holdings in the two suits are better, but still equal, he will take the same action. A presumed preemptive bid which might cause a trump fit of six or seven cards to be established can easily lead to disaster. If the Unusual two notrump bidder does hold the expected suit lengths of at least five-five in the two suits that he expresses, a combined trump length holding in the two hands of eight or more cards will usually be found.

What, then, is the preemptor expected to do at his next turn to bid? No, this question is not a joke!! Misusers of this convention do not understand that a preemptive bid says it all. Once you have preempted, if your message has correctly expressed your hand, you should never feel the need to bid again on that hand.

So, is it possible for a bidder who has jumped to two notrump after an opposing opening bid to take another call without having misdescribed his hand?

The answer is yes. By bidding again he indicates that his call of two notrump was not a preemptive bid at all. He shows a hand at the opposite end of the value range. His further bid will usually be a raise of the suit selected by the Advancer. Instead of having used this convention to preempt in two suits, further action by the two notrump bidder indicates interest in a slam. If responder raises after the Unusual two notrump call and the Advancer passes, with a hand worth a slam try, the overcaller can repeat his notrump takeout at a higher level.

HIGHER LEVEL JUMPS IN NOTRUMP
AFTER AN OPENING ONE BID

The jump to two notrump after an opposing opening bid at the one level is not the only possible jump in notrump. The overcaller can jump to notrump at the three, four, five, or six level. What does each of these jumps indicate?

Three notrump is always to play! When you jump to three notrump after an opposing opening bid, you should have a stopper in the opening bidder's suit, at least one other stopper (preferably in an unbid major suit), and a solid minor suit of seven or more cards which will serve as a source of tricks. Your hand should fit the description of an opening ACOL three notrump bid, but guarantee a stopper in the suit of the opening bid.

Jump overcalls of four, five or six notrump show a need for greater preemption than would have been afforded by a mere jump to two notrump. This should show greater suit lengths as well as virtually no defensive values. The overcaller will be six-five, six-six, or even seven-six in the two suits he has shown. He will choose his level based on several circumstances. These include:

1) The vulnerability. When not vulnerable versus vulnerable opponents, preemption is easiest and most likely to produce good results.

2) If partner is a passed hand, the likelihood that he holds two or more defensive tricks has been decidedly reduced. This adds to the effectiveness of the preemptive action.

3) The longer your suits, the less likelihood that the high cards in them will be able to take tricks defensively.

SUMMARY — JUMP OVERCALLS IN NOTRUMP

I. The jump overcall of two notrump shows five-five or six-five distribution.

   A. It will show either the minor suits, or the two lower ranking unbid suits, based upon partnership agreement.

   B. It will usually be a preemptive bid in two suits.
     1. It will include less than opening bid strength.
     2. It should never include as much as two defensive tricks.
     3. If the hand contains opening bid strength, or two or more defensive tricks, the bidder should overcall rather than use the Unusual jump to two notrump.
     4. Having used the Unusual Notrump to describe his hand entirely, the bidder should not volunteer another bid.

   C. It will sometimes be a slam try in two suits.
     1. To complete his slam try, the Unusual two notrump bidder will raise the suit selected by the Advancer.
     2. If responder raises and Advancer passes, another call in notrump at a higher level indicates that the overcaller was making a slam try.

II. The jump overcall of three notrump is to play.

   A. It shows a hand with a solid minor suit as a source of tricks.

   B. It also shows stoppers in at least two other suits, one of which will be the suit of the opening bid.

Before we move on to other overcalls in notrump, it is time to look at some examples:

♠ 7
♥ 95
♦ KJ986
♣ QJ1085

Here is a classic for the jump to two notrump. The hand meets the requirements of suit lengths and lack of defensive strength, while providing reasonable offensive values. If partner has a three or four card fit for either suit, enough tricks will be produced on offense to offset the possible gain the opponents might make if allowed to play a contract in one of the major suits.

♠ 7
♥ 5
♦ AJ943
♣ AJ8765

This hand is from an article on the Unusual Notrump which appeared in the ACBL *Bulletin* in the July 1995 issue. The author recommends a call of two notrump after an opening bid of one heart.

The suit lengths are fine and the value range is right, but there is one problem with preempting with this hand. It has too much defense! If you use the Unusual Notrump with this hand and the opponents arrive at a game, partner may take a save when the game was going down.

♠ 7
♥ 86
♦ AKJ84
♣ KQJ65

Here is another hand which is too good for the Unusual notrump. With this hand you should overcall in diamonds, and plan to bid clubs later. Again, when you make the error of using the Unusual notrump, if partner has a good fit for one of your suits, he may take a phantom sacrifice against a major suit game.

♠ 73
♥ J4
♦ Q9854
♣ KQJ2

Time and again the undisciplined and uneducated jump to two notrump with a hand such as this. Yes, it does have the right value range, but remember that with two-two or three-three in the minors, partner will bid clubs, and you must pass and play a six or seven card fit, even if doubled for penalties. You have nowhere to go!

♠ A4
♥ —
♦ AQJ95
♣ KQJ983

This hand needs little but a fit to have a play for slam in either minor suit. After a major suit opening bid, jump to two notrump, and raise if partner is able to select a suit. When the opponents preempt to game, try five clubs, even when partner has not been able to speak. If your suits were equal in length your would repeat your notrump takeout at a higher level. Partner will understand your five club call as a slam try with longer clubs than diamonds (at least five-six).

♠ 7
♥ —
♦ KQJ954
♣ QJ10963

Here is a hand with great offense and almost zero defense. Depending on vulnerability and whether or not partner was a passed hand, a tactical choice of four, five, or even six notrump could be right.

♠ K5
♥ A62
♦ 4
♣ AKQJ863

After an opening bid of one spade, this hand is a classic three notrump overcall. When spades are led, they will have to win the ace and be able to shift and win four diamond tricks to beat your contract. When the opening bid is one heart, you should make the same call, but with less assuredness. When hearts are led, you may have only eight tricks.

CHAPTER EIGHT
OTHER OVERCALLS IN NOTRUMP AFTER AN OPPOSING OPENING BID

Some confusion exists regarding when a notrump overcall is natural, and when it is Unusual. When your opponents have bid two suits, it is still possible for you to have a natural overcall in notrump. The fact that your opponents have opened and responded does not negate the fact that your side might be able to make a game.

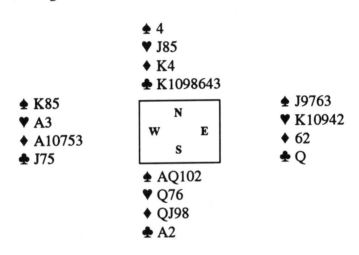

```
                ♠ 4
                ♥ J85
                ♦ K4
                ♣ K1098643
  ♠ K85            N        ♠ J9763
  ♥ A3                      ♥ K10942
  ♦ A10753    W       E     ♦ 62
  ♣ J75            S        ♣ Q
                ♠ AQ102
                ♥ Q76
                ♦ QJ98
                ♣ A2
```

With West opening the bidding one diamond and East responding one spade, South needs to be able to make a natural overcall of one notrump. Looking at a source of tricks in clubs and the well-placed diamond king, North should confidently raise to three notrump. If South were unable to bid one notrump naturally, it would be virtually impossible to reach this iron clad game.

Despite this obvious need, many partnerships have agreed that when the oppponents have bid two suits, their overcall in notrump shows the other two suits, but without the defensive strength to make a takeout double. Should South hold such a hand after the opening bid and response, it is still possible to jump to two notrump, which removes all ambiguity.

However, if South had been the dealer and had passed, there would be no need for him to jump to two notrump to describe a hand with little defense and length in both of the unbid suits. As a passed hand, he could not hold a natural notrump bid, so a simple overcall in notrump without jumping would send his desired message.

The use of an overcall in notrump by an unpassed hand to show the two unbid suits has been christened the "sandwich notrump." Those who decide to play that convention must give up their natural overcall in notrump after an opening bid and a response in a new suit.

The test of the usefulness for any convention should be the measurement of what is gained by its use compared to what is given up for its adoption. Conventions such as Stayman and Lebensohl are standouts, giving up almost nothing to open doors to wonderful worlds of bidding. Not so the "sandwich notrump." It gives up a valuable tool for very little apparent gain.

When the opponents have bid and raised the same suit, the picture changes. In such an auction the prospective bidder is much less likely to have the strength and suit length in the bid and raised suit to want to play a contract in notrump. With most strong balanced hands, he will nearly always have adequate support for the unbid suits which will enable him to compete by making a takeout double. This makes it more reasonable to have the agreement that when the opponents have bid and raised a major suit, a simple overcall of two notrump is Unusual rather than a suggestion that notrump become the final contract.

After a major suit has been bid and raised, the opponent to call may be in the balance position. The balancing bid of two notrump should suggest that the bidder does not want to sell out, but wishes to compete in the lower ranking suits. Here the use of the Unusual Notrump does not require great suit length. Consider a situation like this one:

Opener	You	Responder	Partner
1♠	Pass	2♠	Pass
Pass	??		

You hold:

♠ 8753
♥ 9
♦ KQJ5
♣ AQ103

It is clear that your partner is very short in spades and probably holds several hearts. However, he is likely to have a fit for one of the minor suits. If you reopen with double, he is almost certain to bid hearts, maybe even by jumping to the four level!! Although there was no convenient bid that would have expressed this hand after the opening bid of one spade, a balance of two notrump is just about right to show your values and interest in the minor suits.

After an opening bid and two passes, it is possible to bid notrump, or to jump in notrump in the balancing position. Please do not confuse either of these actions with the Unusual Notrump.

A simple bid in notrump in the balancing position after an opening bid and two passes shows a balanced hand in the range of about ten to fourteen high card points (less than the strength for an opening bid or a natural overcall in notrump). If the balancer does hold a strong opening notrump, when in balance position he describes that hand by first doubling for takeout, then bidding notrump at his next turn.

A jump to two notrump in the balancing position after an opening bid and two passes is not the Unusual Notrump. It shows a balanced hand in the range of nineteen or twenty high card points. This is an illustration of the axiom: "There is no such thing as a weak jump in the balance position!!!"

Let's look again at the situation in which the opponents have opened the bidding and responded in a new suit. When you hold length in the two remaining suits and wish to compete as a passed hand, you may overcall one notrump. However, if unpassed, you should jump to two notrump. If instead you make a takeout double, you still say that you hold the two unbid suits, but the rest of your message is quite different.

A double for takeout in this situation does not promise suit lengths of five-five, but might be made with as few cards in each suit as four. An additional distinction is that this takeout double promises some defensive strength. Your partner will expect at least two defensive tricks.

SUMMARY OF OTHER OVERCALLS IN NOTRUMP — INCLUDING BALANCING ACTIONS

I. An overcall of one notrump by an unpassed hand after the opponents have bid two suits is still a strong notrump. It is not a weak two suited takeout.

    A. A jump overcall in notrump is still Unusual, promising length (at least five-five) in the two unbid suits and denies defensive strength.

    B. A takeout double in such an auction does not promise such great suit length.

        1. It should show at least four-four in the unbid suits.
        2. It promises at least two defensive tricks.

II. An overcall in notrump after the opponents have bid and raised a major suit will be at the two level. It is Unusual, promising both minors, at least five-five, and probably with preemptive values.

III. Notrump bids in the balance position have different meanings.

   A. A balance of one notrump after an opening bid and two passes shows a balanced hand in the range of ten to fourteen high card points. With fifteen to eighteen, the balancer should first double, then bid notrump.

   B. A jump to two notrump after an opening bid and two passes shows a balanced hand with nineteen or twenty high card points.

   C. There is no such thing as a weak jump in the balance position.

Again, it is time for some example hands:

♠ K93
♥ A5
♦ QJ83
♣ J1062

When there has been an opening bid and two passes, with this hand it is almost always right to balance. When the opening bid was in spades, diamonds or clubs, a bid of one notrump will do nicely. When the opening bid was one heart, reopen with double.

♠ KJ975
♥ K4
♦ QJ873
♣ 9

When you have passed as dealer and hear an auction of one club on your left, pass by partner, one heart on your right, you can bid one notrump as a takeout for the two unbid suits without much defense. As an unpassed hand, you would need to jump to two notrump to describe your holdings.

♠ AK953
♥ 84
♦ A10983
♣ 2

You cannot be a passed hand, for you would have opened the bidding. After an opening bid of one club and a response of one heart, you would double with this hand rather than use Unusual Notrump because of your defensive strength.

♠ KJ86
♥ K3
♦ A7643
♣ 87

Whether a passed hand or not, when the auction comes to you with an opening bid of one club on your left, pass by partner, one heart on your right, a double for takeout describes the nature of your hand. You have support for both of the unbid suits, and you also have defense against a contract that the opponents might declare.

♠ AQ5
♥ KQ7
♦ AJ6
♣ KJ87

After an opening bid in any suit at your left and two passes, a jump to two notrump describes this hand. Remember that there are no weak jumps in the balance position.

♠ KQJ963
♥ A4
♦ A943
♣ 3

After an opening bid of one club, one diamond, or one heart on your left, if two passes ensue, jump to two spades. Although this hand has no relation to the Unusual Notrump, it illustrates that a jump in the balance position shows a good hand.

♠ KJ4
♥ QJ83
♦ A96
♣ AJ10

After an opening bid in any suit and two passes, do not bid one notrump! To show that you have an opening one notrump bid, you must first double and then bid in notrump.

Here we end our discussion of the Unusual Notrump shown by a jump in that denomination. We have also discussed satellite auctions so that the differences can be readily understood. We now will move on to see what the Advancer should do in auctions in which his partner has used the Unusual Notrump as it has been described here.

CHAPTER NINE
ADVANCER'S ACTIONS AFTER AN UNUSUAL NOTRUMP OVERCALL

Since the Unusual Notrump expressed by a jump overcall at the two level will usually be made with a hand that is preempting in two suits, the advancer should always begin with the assumption that his partner has a hand of that nature. When the overcall was based on a stronger hand with ambitions for slam, the Advancer will learn that when the overcaller rebids.

With most hands, the Advancer will simply select one of the two suits shown by the jump overcall at the cheapest possible level. When the Advancer has reasonable high card strength, the opener's side may withdraw from the bidding and allow a contract to be played by the Advancer's side at the three level. When the Advancer holds three or four cards in one of the indicated suits, his choice is easy. When his holdings in the two indicated suits are equal in length, he will usually bid the cheapest one. Sometimes the Advancer will need to bid a doubleton.

If the Responder doubles the jump overcall of two notrump, Advancer should speak only when he has a clear preference for one of the Overcaller's suits. The double should carry the message that the Responder has good defense against one or both of the suits shown by the jump overcall in notrump. When the Advancer has no preference for one of the indicated suits over the other, he should pass to allow the jump overcaller to select the suit himself. When the jump overcall has been made on a six-five hand, this allows the six card suit to be named as the prospective trump suit.

When the Advancer has limited values and a good length fit for one of the indicated suits, he should jump preemptively in the suit of that fit. The level to which he jumps should be determined by the vulnerability and how much defensive strength he holds.

If a sacrifice at the five level against an opposing major suit game that seems reasonably sure to make will give up an amount less than the value of the game, Advancer should jump to the five level without giving his opponents more bidding space in which to exchange information. If they decide to bid on over the advance sacrifice, they may be one level too high.

When the Advancer has a good hand and can visualize a game or slam, he can Cue Bid in the opening bidder's suit. Upon hearing this Cue Bid, the jump overcaller should bid as cheaply as possible in a known suit whenever his hand is minimum, or should make some other expressive call when his hand is good within its known limits.

The Advancer may also hold the fourth suit which has not yet been bid or shown. When his holding in that suit makes it self sufficient enough to be the trump suit without any support from partner, he may introduce that suit, overruling the suggestion made by use of the Unusual Notrump overcall. This presentation of the fourth suit as Advancer's choice to be trumps is non-forcing, but with certain hands, the jump overcaller may be able to raise.

A raise of the Unusual Notrump overcall to game indicates that the Advancer holds good values, fits with one or both of the suits shown by the use of Unusual Notrump, and stoppers in the two remaining suits, particularly in the suit of the opening bid.

Let us look at more examples:

♠ A965
♥ QJ863
♦ 94
♣ 76

After an opening bid of one spade, your partner has made a jump overcall of two notrump. Without betraying your fear of suffering a potentially large penalty, bid three clubs. Even though your opponents may have six trumps to your seven, they may let you get away unscathed. When Responder has doubled two notrump, pass to let your partner make his choice of trump suits.

♠ A953
♥ QJ863
♦ 4
♣ 976

In the same auction, your choice is made easy. Even when Responder doubles, bid three clubs to show your clear choice between the two suits your partner has shown.

♠ A95
♥ QJ863
♦ 4
♣ J976

With almost no defense against a spade game by the opposition and an excellent fit for one of partner's suits, at all but unfavorable vulnerability you should jump to five clubs. When not vulnerable against vulnerable opponents, you might even consider jumping to six clubs, hoping to have a chance to defeat six spades.

♠ A953
♥ AKJ5
♦ 4
♣ KQ102

In the same auction, with this hand Advancer might Cue Bid three spades to indicate his interest in slam in one of the suits shown by the Unusual Notrump jump overcall. When the overcaller reacts to the Cue Bid by bidding four clubs (his cheapest escape), you will settle for a club game. If he offers any encouragement by making another call, drive to a club slam.

♠ KQ10
♥ AQ5
♦ K754
♣ AJ2

With this hand Advancer should raise to three notrump. With potential double stoppers in each danger suit and fits for both of partner's minor suits, nine tricks at notrump looks quite probable.

♠ 7
♥ AKJ10754
♦ Q65
♣ K3

Despite your knowledge that partner is five-five or longer in the minor suits, your heart suit should be trumps. When vulnerable, jump to four hearts as partner will surely have reasonable minor suit high cards.

CHAPTER TEN
UNUSUAL NOTRUMP AFTER HIGH LEVEL OPENING BIDS

Overcalls in notrump, when the opposition has opened the bidding at the two level or higher, are normally strong balanced hands. When the opening bid has been a weak two bid, the overcall of two notrump shows a strong balanced hand in the range of about fifteen to nineteen high card points. A jump to three notrump is usually of the ACOL variety.

When the opening two bid is strong, however, the overcall of two notrump is understood as Unusual. The tournament player will rarely encounter opponents who use natural strong two bids, but when that rare situation does exist, an overcall in notrump shows the two lower ranking of the remaining suits.

Most tournament players today use weak or conventional two bids in diamonds, and natural weak two bids in the major suits. Their strong forcing opening bid is an artificial bid of two clubs. The Unusual Notrump overcall to show two suits can be used directly over the two club opening bid, or after that opening bid and a response, which might be either conventional or natural. The overcall of two notrump should be Unusual, showing the two lowest suits which have not been bid naturally.

When your opponents have opened at the three level, three notrump is always to play. A jump to four notrump over an opposing opening three bid can be played as Unusual.

The higher the level of the opening bid, the less likely that double is meant for takeout. Doubles of opening high level bids are usually based on hands with good defensive values, but not a stack in the suit of the preemptive opening bidder. When the partner of the doubler removes the double to a suit of his own, he does not do so for fear that the doubled contract will make. Instead he feels that the high cards shown by his partner's double will give him a good enough dummy to make his own high level contract.

Opening bids in major suits at the four level are usually based on long and strong suits. Double of a four heart opening bid shows good high card strength, but it promises that the doubler has some support, or at least tolerance for the spade suit. Double of an opening bid of four spades simply shows great strength without promising support for any particular suit.

When an opening bid of four spades is doubled and the Advancer removes to a lower ranking suit at the five level, his message is that he expects to win eleven tricks, not that he fears four spades will make. If the doubler's hand is well suited to offense in the Advancer's suit, and if his values are greater than the minimum he might have been expected to hold, the doubler has license to raise the Advancer to a slam. In short, the removal of a doubled major suit contract at the four level to the Advancer's suit at the five level is a mild slam try.

For the reasons just expressed, a bid of four notrump after an opening bid at the four level in either major suit is for takeout. It should be an Unusual Notrump with a very good hand. When the opening bid has been four hearts, the call of four notrump shows both minor suits. When the opening bid has been four spades, the Unusual Notrump takeout is usually three suited. The exception is the hand which holds both red suits without support for clubs. When the four notrump takeout after an opening bid of four spades has brought forth a five club call from the Advancer, when the Overcaller then bids five diamonds he shows that he holds a red two suiter rather than the expected three suited hand for his takeout.

Some examples:

♠ AJ84
♥ A5
♦ KQJ6
♣ A83

After an opposing opening bid of four hearts, this hand should double. Unless the opening bidder has no losers in diamonds, the high card strength here is enough to defeat most four heart opening bids. One key to this call is the good spade support, which is part of the requisite holding for doubling the opening bid of four hearts. One would not expect to hold this hand and hear an opening bid of four spades, but this hand would happily double that opening bid for penalties as well.

When after having doubled an opening four bid in either major suit, you hear a call of five clubs from the Advancer, you should consider raising to slam. If the Advancer instead removed to five diamonds, you should Cue Bid the opener's major suit to show interest in a grand slam.

♠ 6
♥ 3
♦ KQJ98
♣ AQJ753

After an opening bid of two clubs, after an artifical response to a two club opening bid, or after a natural response in a major suit, bid two notrump with this hand. This action is reasonably safe at almost any vulnerability. This hand should also call four notrump over an opening bid of four hearts.

♠ —
♥ AQJ8
♦ KQ1097
♣ AK85

This is a classic hand for a takeout of four notrump after an opening bid of four spades. You are happy with the trump suit that your partner selects, whatever it may be.

♠ 8
♥ AKQ74
♦ KQ10853
♣ 5

After an opening bid of four spades, you should also make a takeout call of four notrump with this hand. If partner bids five clubs, your correction to five diamonds offers him a choice of the red suits.

CHAPTER ELEVEN
OTHER SITUATIONS FOR THE USE OF UNUSUAL NOTRUMP

Several other auctions may arise which use the Unusual Notrump. Most of these will be recognized through the application of simple logic. Several such auctions appear in the *Encyclopedia of Bridge*. However, due to the necessity of presentations which are brief summaries, virtually no examples are presented there. We will examine those auctions here and provide examples as well.

There are only a few auctions in which after opening the bidding, when the opener makes a subsequent call in notrump, that call suggests notrump as the contract he is seeking. In the auction: 1♣ - Pass - Pass - 1♠, 1NT, or: 1♣ - 1♠ - Pass - Pass, 1NT, opener shows a balanced hand with eighteen or nineteen high card points (and spades stopped, of course). Except for this particular strength range, opener with a strong balanced hand will have opened in notrump, or rebid notrump after having opened with two clubs.

With this being the exception, unexpected calls in notrump by an opening bidder or by an overcaller are used to convey a different message. This form of Unusual Notrump will be used to express the desire to compete with a two suited hand, but without the ability to bid the second suit conveniently. His reason for not being able to bid the second suit will usually be one of these:

1) A rebid in the second suit will send the incorrect message that the two suits are equal, or nearly equal in length. In fact, most such uses are based on six-four, seven-four, or seven-five patterns.

2) A rebid in the second suit will carry the auction to a higher level than is desired. The Unusual Notrump call to show the second (lesser) suit will allow a choice without forcing the auction to the higher level that would be necessary if the bidder had to reverse to show his second suit.

♠ 7
♥ K4
♦ AJ108
♣ AQJ753

After an opening bid of one spade, you have overcalled two clubs. Responder has raised to two spades, and after two passes it is your turn to call. In order to compete further, your most descriptive bid is two notrump.

This should not be misinterpreted as an offer to play in notrump. If you truly wished to play in notrump, your first overcall would have been one notrump rather than two clubs.

Partner should understand you have a good club suit that you might have rebid. However, your call of two notrump says that you also hold a four card diamond suit. Your partner is asked to bid diamonds when he holds four or more of that suit and otherwise to return to three clubs. Note that your second suit in this example cannot be hearts. With the good club suit you are known to hold, when you also held four hearts your first call would have been a Top and Bottom Cue Bid.

♠ A5
♥ —
♦ AQJ7
♣ KQJ10752

You have opened the bidding with one club, planning to reverse to diamonds at your rebid. Your plans go awry, however, when your left hand opponent overcalls with one heart, partner passes, and Right hand opponent raises preemptively to four hearts.

Four notrump is the call that allows you to show that in addition to your good club suit, you also hold four diamonds. Again partner is asked to bid diamonds with four or more of them; otherwise, he should return to five clubs.

```
♠ A5            ♠ A5
♥ AQJ7          ♥ 3
♦ KQJ1075       ♦ KQJ1075
♣ 3             ♣ AQJ7
```

As you can see, these two hands are the same with hearts and clubs interchanged. Holding either of these hands, you open by bidding one diamond and hear an overcall of one spade. After partner passes your right hand opponent raises to four spades. With either of these hands you can compete further by bidding four notrump.

Partner will know that you have excellent diamonds and also a second suit which is probably only four cards long. When he holds four or more clubs, he will next bid five clubs. When your hand is the second one above, you will be content to play in clubs, but with the first hand you should correct to five diamonds.

The five diamond correction will indicate that your second suit was not clubs, but rather that it was hearts. Partner will bid on to five hearts when in addition to clubs, he also holds four or more cards in the heart suit.

When partner bids five diamonds, indicating that he holds fewer than four cards in the club suit (since he is known to hold only one spade, two at most on a bad day), he is almost certain to hold four or more hearts and you can correct to that suit.

```
♠ 7
♥ 5
♦ QJ954
♣ J106432
```

The auction begins with one heart from partner and an overcall of one spade. Since you are too weak for a negative double, you pass, and after left hand opponent raises to two spades, two passes follow and it is your turn again. A call of two notrump at this point shows that you have a weak hand with a minor two-suiter.

♠ —
♥ J5
♦ KQ1095
♣ A107654

After you pass as dealer, left hand opponent preempts with a call of three spades. Your partner doubles for takeout and right hand opponent passes. A call of four notrump by you shows a minor two suiter with values enough to play a game in this auction.

♠ —
♥ KQ653
♦ AJ983
♣ 972

This is one of the three hands shown in the Encyclopedia. Your partner opens by bidding one club and your right hand opponent overcalls four spades. Credit is given to Sidney Silidor who suggested that a call of four notrump at this point should show this hand.

* *

You should remember that when notrump is bid and it is entirely unlikely that the bidder wishes to play a contract in notrump, logic dictates that the opposite meaning should apply. The Unusual bid in notrump should show some two suited hand that could be consistent with the messages of the previous auction.

PART THREE

TWO SUITED
DEFENSES

CHAPTER TWELVE
DEFENSES TO OPPONENTS' OPENING NOTRUMP BIDS

Attempting to present all of the available two suited defenses to an opposing notrump opening bid is a formidable task. Our research goes beyond the normal sources and attempts to cover all of the suggested defenses of consequence that are available at the time of this writing. We hope to be as complete as possible, but cannot guarantee that we have managed to cover all of the possibilities.

We have tried to group the defenses against opposing notrump bids which are similar and to list them in historical order.

1. LANDY

The defense suggested by Alvin Landy, who was Executive Secretary of the American Contract Bridge League from 1950 until his death in 1967, may well be the first attempt to offer the opportunity to show two suits. The Landy convention uses a bid of two clubs to show the major suits after an opposing opening bid of one notrump.

The two club bid promises at least four-four in the major suits, although there is a variation promising at least five hearts and four spades. With most mundane hands, Advancer bids his longer major suit holding at the two level. If he must bid a three card suit, he hopes that he has found a five card holding in the hand of the convention user.

Without a fit for either major suit, Advancer does have some options. If Advancer has a weak hand with long clubs, he may pass the conventional takeout call of two clubs. When he elects to bid two diamonds, that call is natural and non forcing. A bid of three diamonds is natural and encouraging, but non forcing.

A jump to three of either major suit is natural and invitational, and will often be made with a three card holding, assuming that the user of the convention will usually hold five cards, rather than just four, in each major. A jump to four of a major suit shows good values and a good fit for the major suit. Advancer expects to make a game even when the convention user holds only four cards in the suit in which he jumps to game.

Using the Landy convention, double is for the major suits by a passed hand so that a bid of two clubs can be natural.

There is disagreement in the authoritative sources concerning Landy. *The Encyclopedia of Bridge* states that the only forcing response to seek further information is a bid of three clubs by the Advancer. This bid has no relation to the club suit, but shows a very good hand and asks the Landy bidder to describe further. The Encyclopedia says that a response of two notrump is natural and encouraging.

In *Bridge Conventions Complete*, Amalya Kearse says that two notrump is forcing and seeks further information. This point of disagreement will probably never be resolved, since Landy left no written presentation. Landy's value is more historical than practical since the flood of new ideas has produced many two suited conventions to be used against an opposing notrump opening bid. However, Landy first opened the door to the idea that such defenses were viable and, perhaps, even essential in today's tournament world.

2. RIPSTRA

J.G. Ripstra expanded on the idea presented by Landy to suggest that a bid in either minor suit shows both major suits, but that the call be made in the bidder's longer minor suit. In the eyes of some users, this presented not a two suited, but rather a three suited takeout to be used as a weapon to defend after an opposing opening bid of one notrump.

Although the minor suit bid presumably offered a third possible place to play, if the bidder held five-five in the major suits, he might also hold only a doubleton in his longer minor suit. This fact made the choice of playing in the minor suit much less attractive.

The Ripstra "improvement" on Landy became popular and had a strong following until later conventions supplanted both of these early entries in the favor of tournament players.

3. BECKER

The next logical step in showing two suits was to show the minors as well as majors. The convention popularly known as Becker uses an overcall of two clubs to show both minor suits, and two diamonds to show both majors. We have heard that no member of this prestigeous bridge family claims credit for the convention, although the name ascribed to it would seem to indicate its source.

The Encyclopedia listing suggests that the user of the convention should have five-five in the suits shown, but mentions that at matchpoint duplicate users will often have five-four. It also states that the user will have limited high card strength, since there had been no double for penalties.

4. ASTRO

This convention combined the thinking of three experts, whose names furnished an acronym which identified the convention. The three were Allinger, Stern, and Rossler. Their idea was to provide two-suited takeouts in which there was a known anchor suit, and another unknown suit which was promised by use of the convention.

An overcall of the opening notrump bid in clubs promised hearts (the anchor suit), as well as a minor suit which at that point had not been identified. An overcall of two diamonds promised spades (the anchor suit) and any one of the remaining suits.

Advancer was able to bid the anchor suit when holding three or more cards in that suit and a moderate hand. He could also jump in the known suit to bid or invite a game whenever he held good values and four or more cards in that suit.

When he held fewer than three cards in the anchor suit,

Advancer could bid in the neutral suit (the suit between the takeout call and the anchor suit) whenever he held three or more cards in that suit and two or fewer in the anchor suit. Pass by the Advancer would show at least six cards in the suit bid, no interest in the anchor suit, and only moderate values at most.

Whenever the Advancer held good values and needed further information, he could bid two notrump. This was a forcing call designed to have the ASTRO bidder describe his hand further.

5. ASPRO

Terrence Reese, the British expert, undertook to improve on ASTRO, and named his variation after a popular British aspirin. Reese imaginatively called the overcaller the astronaut and introduced the idea of a relay to allow further description.

To show a hand with five spades and four or five hearts, the astronaut bids two clubs, and after a relay of two diamonds bids two spades. When the astronaut holds only four spades and five hearts, he begins with two clubs and then bids hearts when he has limited values. With a better hand he starts with two diamonds, then bids two notrump to show a hand of this shape.

With two suiters of six-five or six-six distribution, specific bids indicate the two suits held. A bid of two notrump shows black suits, three clubs shows minor suits, three diamonds shows red suits, and three hearts shows major suits. With other combinations (clubs and hearts, or diamonds and spades), the bidder first bids two clubs, then jumps in his nearest six card suit.

6. ASPTRO

This rarely used variation borrows from both of the presentations above. Two clubs shows hearts and another suit, while two diamonds shows spades and another suit.

7. GRAN0-ASTRO

This is yet another variation on the above. Double shows spades and another suit, while a minor suit overcall shows the suit bid and hearts. This variation is ascribed to Matt Granovetter.

8. PINPOINT ASTRO

This is a variation of the BROZEL convention which allows for the expression of specific suits. In this variation, double is used to show a single suited hand, and two suited hands are shown as follows: Two clubs shows clubs and hearts; two diamonds shows diamonds and hearts; two hearts shows hearts and spades; two spades shows spades and a minor suit; two notrump shows both minors.

9. ROTH-STONE ASTRO

The idea attached to this conventional usage is to show even more two suited combinations. Instead of focusing on the heart suit at the two level, the focal suit is spades. Here are the combinations shown: Two clubs shows clubs and spades; two diamonds shows diamonds and spades; three clubs shows clubs and hearts; three diamonds shows diamonds and hearts; double shows hearts and spades.

10. BROZEL

The BROZEL convention combines many of the preceding ideas. Double is used to show a single suited hand with good values, and the Advancer is encouraged to pass and defend if he has reasonable values. When he is unable to defend, he bids two clubs to allow the doubler to show his good single suit.

Two suited takeouts are made at the two level as follows: Two clubs shows clubs and hearts; two diamonds shows diamonds and hearts; two hearts shows hearts and spades; two spades shows spades and a minor suit — a bid of two notrump by

Advancer would ask for the minor suit to be designated; two notrump shows both minor suits.

A jump to the three level shows a good three suited hand. The bidder jumps in his short suit, promising at least four cards in each of the unbid suits.

11. CANSINO

This variation by another British expert uses an overall of two clubs to show clubs and any other two suits, and an overcall of two diamonds to show both major suits.

Up to this point in our discussion, we have looked at conventional ideas which have been around for several years. Although several of these conventional ideas are sound enough to have endured, more modern thoughts have taken over in recent times, and the following conventions are more popular at the time of this writing.

12. SUCTION

This convention is used to show one or two suiters. The bidder makes his call so that the Advancer will bid the next higher ranking suit. When the bidder holds a one suited hand, he will pass or raise. When the bidder holds a two suited hand and his two suits are touching, he then bids the next higher ranking suit. When he continues in this fashion, he shows the suit he has bid and the suit which ranks directly above that suit. Therefore:

An overcall of two clubs shows either diamonds or hearts and spades;
An overcall of two diamonds shows either hearts or spades and clubs;
An overcall of two hearts shows either spades or clubs and diamonds;
An overcall of two spades shows either clubs or diamonds and hearts.

This approach is usually supplemented by the use of double and two notrump to show specific non-touching two suiters (spades and diamonds, or hearts and clubs).

This defense can also be employed against a system which uses a strong and artificial one club opening bid.

13. WOOLSEY

The conventional approach designed by Kit Woolsey allows for competition with two suited hands, but makes a strong attempt to convey suit lengths in the hand of the overcaller. Here are the parameters of this convention:

1) Double promises a four card major suit and a longer minor suit.
2) Two clubs shows both major suits.
3) Two diamonds shows a single suited major suit hand.
4) Two hearts or two spades promises five or more cards in the major suit bid, as well as a four card or longer minor suit.
5) Two notrump shows both minors or any gigantic two suiter.
6) Three clubs or three diamonds is natural.

Continuing auctions are as follows:

When the intruder has doubled, showing a four card major and a longer minor suit, the Advancer can:

a) Bid two clubs to ask for the minor suit. The doubler can either pass to show clubs, or correct to two diamonds. When the doubler does bid two diamonds, a bid of two hearts by Advancer asks him to pass with hearts, or to bid two spades with spades.

b) Bid two diamonds. This asks the doubler to show his major suit.

c) Bid either two hearts or two spades. This shows a suit held by the Advancer and seeks no information about what the doubler's suits might be.

d) If after Advancer bids two diamonds and the doubler shows his major suit, Advancer next bids two notrump, he shows a good hand with a fit for the doubler's major suit. The doubler is asked to bid game in the major suit with a good hand, or return to the major at the three level with a lesser hand.

e) Bid two notrump. This promises a fit for the major suit (Advancer must be at least four-four in the majors) and is a general game try. With a good hand, the doubler will bid either three notrump or his minor suit, whichever is more descriptive. With a poor hand for the auction, the doubler will retreat to his major suit at the three level.

When the competitive bid is instead a call of two clubs showing both major suits, Advancer's bid of two diamonds asks for the longer or better major. Other advances are natural.

After the overcall of two diamonds showing a major single suiter, two hearts by the Advancer asks for a pass or conversion to spades — Advancer can be weak in hearts or strong in spades. Two spades by Advancer asks for pass or conversion to three hearts — Advancer can be weak in spades, but willing to play hearts at least at the three level. Two notrump by the Advancer shows a very good hand and asks the overcaller to bid one under his suit to put the opening bidder on lead.

After an overcall of two of a major suit, two notrump by the Advancer asks for overcaller's minor suit, a raise is invitational, and anything else is to play.

Against weak notrump opening bids big hands are shown as follows:

1) Two notrump shows a strong notrump opening bid.
2) Two diamonds followed by two notrump shows a balanced nineteen or twenty points.
3) Double followed by two notrump shows a balanced 21 or 22 points.

In summarizing the strengths and weaknesses of this convention, Kit Woolsey presents the following:

Advantages:

(1) Ability to enter with all two suiters.

(2) Ability to distinguish lengths when showing two suiters.

(3) Ability to stop at two of a minor with minor-major two-suiters.

(4) Ability to put the opener on lead in most cases after an overcall based on a long major.

Disadvantages:

(1) Loss of the penalty double.

(2) Inability to play two of a minor with a one-suiter.

14. BERGEN (also known as DONT)

This defense uses a double to show a single suited hand which is usually not spades. Advancer responds by bidding two clubs and then the doubler can show his suit.

Direct bids in suits are all used to show two suited hands as follows:

Two clubs shows clubs and a higher ranking suit; two diamonds shows diamonds and one of the majors; two hearts shows hearts and spades; two spades shows spades.

15. JUMP BALL

In this conventional application, double asks Advancer to bid two clubs. When this has happened, doubler's continuations are as follows: Pass shows clubs; two diamonds shows red suits; two hearts shows major suits; two spades shows spades with a good hand.

When instead the intruder bids two clubs, he shows either diamonds, or clubs and a major suit. Advancer bids diamonds, and recognizes the message if the overcaller bids on in a major suit. The hand that gets lost is a spade-diamond two suiter.

Bids in major suits are natural. A bid of two spades is merely competitive and not forward going.

16. MECKWELL

The convention designed and used by Jeff Meckstroth and Eric Rodwell is quite simple:

1) Double shows a minor single suiter or both major suits.
2) An overcall of two clubs shows clubs and a major suit.
3) An overcall of two diamonds shows diamonds and a major suit.

17. CAPPELLETTI, HAMILTON, or HELMS

Here we have a convention which is ascribed to three different possible creators. Most of the world knows the claims of Cappelletti and Hamilton, but few know that Jerry Helms also claims to have originated this convention. We feel that this particular convention against an opposing opening bid of one notrump should be given preeminence over most of the others at the time of the writing of this text. We have two specific reasons for this recommendation:

1. It is easy to agree with a new partner. It is reasonably well-known to most tournament players today, and it is a reasonably sound convention.

2. It does not give up the precious penalty double to some artificial purpose, as do many of the conventions which have previously been described. Experience has proved to this writer that loss of the penalty double, even against practitioners of opening strong notrump opening bids, can be disastrous.

Let us define this convention.

1) Double is for penalties, suggesting a strong balanced hand behind the opening notrump bidder. The doubler should hold high cards in the range that matches or exceeds the top of the notrump range being doubled. Caution!! When you have a very good hand of about twenty points or more and you double for penalties, your partner will rarely have values enough to pass.

An alternate hand for the double is a source of tricks in a long and strong suit, and early stoppers in at least two other suits.

Something like a suit of KQJ10xx and two side aces would be typical.

Since the double will usually show a strong balanced hand, we recommend that the Advancer, whenever he is unable to pass for penalties, use the conventional system that would apply when the doubler had opened by bidding one notrump. Two clubs would still be Stayman, two diamonds and two hearts would still be transfers, etc.

2) An overcall of two clubs shows some single suited hand. Usually this will be a suit of six or more cards, but on occasion, one may need to make this call with a reasonable five card suit, simply in order to get into the auction. Advancer is asked to bid two diamonds artificially, which will allow the overcaller to name his suit at his next turn.

When the overcall of two clubs is doubled, Advancer need not bid at all. When he does bid, he shows a good suit of his own, even when his bid is two diamonds, the suit he was asked to temporize in if there had been no double.

3) When the overcaller bids two diamonds, he promises both major suits. He should ideally be five-five for this call, but on a more practical basis, he will often be five-four.

4) When the overcaller bids either two hearts or two spades, he shows the suit bid and also one of the minor suits. When the Advancer has no tolerance for the major suit, he can bid two notrump to ask the overcaller to name his minor suit.

5) As in most defenses, when the overcall is two notrump, this bid shows both minor suits.

6) As a passed hand, when one doubles he cannot hold the values to seek a penalty. For this reason, double of a one notrump opening bid by a passed hand asks the Advancer to bid clubs. It makes no sense for the overcaller with a club suit to need to bid two clubs to indicate that he holds a one suited hand, then bid clubs again at the three level.

When a passed hand doubles the opening bid of one notrump and the Advancer bids two clubs as requested, he should pass with a club suit. When he continues by bidding two diamonds, he indicates that his hand is two suited with diamonds and hearts. He again takes advantage of the fact that his passed hand double cannot be misunderstood as being for penalties. When he holds diamonds and hearts, he does not need to bid two hearts to show his major-minor two suiter and wind up at the three level when diamonds, rather than hearts, is the trump suit that needs to be played. This also allows the Advancer to understand that when a passed hand overcalls two hearts to show hearts and a minor suit, the minor suit will be known to be clubs, since hearts and diamonds is shown in a different way.

7) A facet of this convention which should be understood, but is not widely known is the use of "Exclusion Doubles" after an overcaller has bid two clubs to show a single suited hand, and some action is taken by the responder to the opening notrump bid. After the two club call, responder may bid a major suit at the two level naturally, or may systemically be able to make a transfer bid despite the interfering two club call. When this occurs, the Advancer may wish to urge his partner to compete further and introduce the unknown suit that was announced when the artifical two club call was made.

When the Advancer is short in the suit of the Responder, he will have some sort of fit for each of the other three suits. In order to show this fact to the Overcaller, the Advancer will double responder's call. Double at this point in the auction carries this message: "Partner, they have competed by bidding (or showing) my short suit, and I have support for your suit no matter which of the remaining suits it may be. Please bid on, and you will find an adequate dummy." It is important to understand this adjunct to the use of this popular convention. If either the Overcaller or the Advancer is not aware what "double" means in this auction, a disaster is very possible.

This convention, as previously stated, is probably the best of the modern conventions available, but it does have a weakness. When the would be intruder has a good major suit, he must bid two clubs rather than name his suit at once. This loses the opportunity to block the opponents out of the auction, which should be one of the goals of a bidder who holds a good major suit and hears an opening bid of one notrump by his right hand opponent. Recognizing this problem, one theorist set out to solve it. The result was:

18. HELMS II

Jerry Helms took the problem into consideration, and came up with a simple but effective solution. He interchanged the meanings of an immediate bid of two in a major suit and a bid of two clubs followed by a rebid in a major suit. He determined that the immediate bid of two in a major suit should show a single suited hand in that major. With a major-minor two suiter, the overcaller could first bid two clubs, and then follow by bidding two of his major suit. When the Advancer had no tolerance for the major suit, he could still bid two notrump to locate the minor suit held by the overcaller.

19. HELLO

This logical pattern of thinking led Jerry Helms to believe that there was still a better idea which could be developed. With his regular partner (Bill Lohman) he developed a further conventional approach which they have agreed to call HELLO. Here are the facets of this improved convention:

1) Double is still for penalties.
2) An overcall of two clubs shows either a diamond suit, or a major-minor two suiter. When the Advancer wishes to ask for the minor suit, he bids two notrump.
3) An overcall of two diamonds is a transfer to hearts.
4) An overcall of two hearts shows both major suits.
5) An overcall of two spades shows spades(!!).
6) An overcall of two notrump shows clubs.
7) An overcall of three clubs shows both minor suits.
8) An overcall of three diamonds shows both major suits with a very good hand.

We believe this to be the best convention available at this time to show various combinations of suits.

DEFENDING AGAINST AN OVERCALL OF ONE NOTRUMP

When your partner has opened in a suit at the one level and an opponent has overcalled by bidding one notrump (unless that overcall is conventional), it shows an opening one notrump bid in the approximate range of fourteen to eighteen high card points. It also promises a stopper in the suit of the opening bid. Responder indicates that he holds good values by doubling the overcall for penalties.

When responder bids a new suit, that call is natural and non-forcing. Responder will have at least five cards in his suit, and will not have adequate values to inflict a sizeable penalty on the overcaller.

Since most tournament players today use a five card major system in first and second seats, the opening bidder will frequently hold a four card major suit when he opens the bidding with one of a minor. When responder holds major suits, there needs to be some way to find a major suit fit after the overcall of one notrump.

The earliest solution to this problem was a convention known as "Same Suit Stayman." Credit for the invention of the tool was given to the late Victor Mitchell, so many instead call it "Mitchell Stayman."

When partner has opened the bidding in a minor suit, if you want to raise that minor after the overcall of one notrump, showing support at the two level does nothing to disrupt the opposing auction. The Advancer will often hold a weak hand with a five or six card major suit. When you raise your partner's minor suit to the two level, the Advancer will have an easy entry into the auction to show his long suit.

For this reason, when you truly wish to raise your partner's minor suit opening bid, you need to jump to the three level. Of course, you would not want to raise unless you held at least five card support, since the opening bid in either clubs or diamonds will often be made on a three card holding. The raise to the three level shows your limited values and excellent fit and tends to preempt against the Advancer.

Since a raise of partner's minor suit will be made at the three level, when you do bid that suit at the two level, instead of raising naturally, you are artificially showing major suits. Ideally, you should be five-five in the major suits, but sometimes you will feel a tactical need to show major suits with as little as four-four. It is this call which has been named, "Same Suit Stayman."

Experimentation has shown that some of the best conventions to be used after an opposing opening bid of one notrump will also function well after an opposing overcall of one notrump. Consider the use of Cappelletti/Hamilton/Helms after partner opens the bidding with one heart and there is an overcall of one notrump:

1) Two clubs says that you have a suit of your own in which to play. Partner is asked to bid two diamonds and then you will name your suit.

2) Two diamonds shows both major suits. Since partner has shown a five card or longer heart suit, your call need show only three card support for hearts, but will promise also that you have spades.

3) Two hearts shows hearts and a minor suit. Again your heart holding need be only three cards, but partner will know that you also have a five card or longer minor suit.

4) Two spades shows that you have spades and a minor suit. This will deny a heart fit. It allows partner to pass and let you play in spades whenever he has a fit for that suit, or to bid two notrump to get you to identify your minor suit.

Let us do another simulation using HELLO after an opening minor suit bid and a overcall of one notrump. Partner opens by bidding one club and the opponent next to speak bids one notrump. Using this convention, your competitive calls are as follows:

1) Two clubs shows that you either have a diamond suit, or that you hold a major-minor two suited hand. Partner is expected to bid two diamonds and await developments.
2) Two diamonds shows that you have a heart suit. Partner can bid that suit confidently if he holds three or more hearts, and can seek a safe haven holding a heart doubleton.
3) Two hearts shows both major suits. Partner can bid either major with a length holding, and can even jump with a good offensive hand, hoping that game might be possible.
4) Two spades is natural. Even without a good fit, partner is able to pass. When he holds a good fit, he can raise preemptively to block the possible following auction. The two spade bidder will not have good values, for if he did, he would have doubled the overcall in notrump.
5) Two notrump shows a fit for clubs. This fit will usually be of five or more cards, since responder realizes that the opening bid might have been made on a three card holding.
6) Three clubs shows both a club fit and a diamond suit as well. Responder will be distributional with long clubs and long diamonds.
7) Three diamonds is a game try showing both major suits. When the opening bidder has a four card major and a sound opening bid, he is encouraged to jump to game in his major suit.

The conventions available as a defense to an opening bid of one notrump can also be used to defend against an overcall of one notrump with little adaptation. The adaptations are logical and you can discuss them briefly with your partner.

CHAPTER THIRTEEN
DEFENSES AGAINST FORCING CLUB OPENING BIDS

When the opponents open the bidding with one club, artificial and forcing, there is need for some defensive agreements. These same agreements can also be used against the mainstream who use two clubs as their forcing opening bid. The need is not as strong against two clubs, since the one club opening bid usually shows sixteen or more points in high cards, while the opening bid of two clubs is usually based on twenty two or more high card points, or nine or more tricks in the hand of the opening bidder.

When the forcing opening bid is one club, there is no clear indication that the hand belongs to the opening bidder's side. Interference when possible is the best defense against a forcing club, since against interference it may be difficult for the opening bidder to show his hand, particularly when it is two suited.

The general rule in defending against a forcing club system is simple: bid if you can. Any interference after the forcing club opening bid may be enough to throw the opening bidder and his partner off stride, and either keep them from finding the right denomination or the right level.

Inevitably, defenses which can show two suited hands are going to develop against this systemic approach. We will examine those which are currently available and appear to be effective when employed against those who use forcing club systems.

1. MATHE

The defense known as Mathe is quite simple and easy to play with a new partner. Double is used to show both major suits, and an overcall of one notrump is used to show both minor suits. With single suited hands an overcall or a jump overcall should be made whenever possible. The jump overcall will show a good suit at least six cards long. With longer suits, the overcaller should do as much as possible to interfere before the opening one club bidder can be given the opportunity to mention a suit. If he began with two suits to mention, the interference may completely deprive him of the opportunity to show his hand.

2. TRUSCOTT

In the defense against a forcing club opening bid devised by Alan Truscott, bids at the one level show two suited hands. Jump overcalls show natural one suited hands. Two suited takeouts are as follows:

1) One diamond shows diamonds and hearts.
2) One heart shows hearts and spades.
3) One spade shows spades and clubs.
4) Two clubs shows clubs and diamonds.
5) Double shows clubs and hearts.
6) One notrump shows spades and diamonds.

3. SUCTION

As a defense against an artificial one club opening bid, the convention known as Suction works much the same way as it does against an opening bid of one notrump. Overcalls are as follows:

1) An overcall of one diamond shows hearts, or spades and clubs.
2) An overcall of one heart shows spades, or clubs and diamonds.
3) An overcall of one spade shows clubs, or diamonds and hearts.
4) An overcall of two clubs shows diamonds, or hearts and spades.

As in the defense against opening bids of one notrump, double and the overcall of one notrump are used to show the non-touching two suited combinations (diamonds and spades, or clubs and hearts).

4. EXCLUSION

This defense uses overcalls as either natural, or to show three suits with shortness in the bid suit. Holding fewer than three cards in the suit of the Overcaller, Advancer treats the call as natural. With three or more cards in the suit, Advancer assumes that the overcall was an Exclusion call, showing the other three suits and seeks another suit in which to play.

5. IDAK (or IDAC)

The Acronym stands for Instant Destroyer and Killer, or Instant Destruction Against a Club. Bids against an artificial one club opening or after a response to an artificial one club opening bid are as follows:

1) With a one suited hand, bid the suit below it at the appropriate level. This is meant as a transfer, but may be passed if you have bid your partner's long suit. If you have transferred and then bid again, you show a two suited hand.
2) With four-three-three-three distribution or with long spades, bid one spade. Without a fit for spades, partner will bid his longest suit knowing that a fit will be found.
3) A jump in spades shows the minor suits.
4) Double shows any three suited hand. Facing the double, Advancer's actions are:

   a) With a one suited hand, he bids two suits below his suit. The doubler can either bid that suit with a fit, or can pass.
   b) With both major suits and a desire to preempt, Advancer bids two notrump. Since the doubler is three suited, a fit is guaranteed.
   c) With both minor suits and a desire to preempt, Advancer bids three notrump.

d) When Advancer has a constructive hand, he bids one notrump. The doubler then bids suits up the line.

e) When Advancer has a two suiter with either spades and diamonds, or with hearts and clubs, he jumps. He knows there is a fit in at least one of his suits.

6. WONDER BIDS

Wonder bids are used in conjunction with IDAK. Vulnerability is the factor which determines which is used. When not vulnerable, IDAK applies; when vulnerable, Wonder Bids are preferred. The parameters for this usage are as follows:

1) A non-jump is natural, or shows a short suit with a three suited hand.

   a) A response in notrump shows a four card fit for the suit of the wonder bid. Advancer can carry on if his call was natural, or can play in notrump if his bid showed a short suit.

   b) With a tolerance for the bid suit in case it is natural, Advancer can bid any new suit at the two level with four or more cards in that suit.

   c) If doubled, the wonder bidder redoubles for takeout when his bid has been in a short suit.

2) Double shows the major suits.

3) An overcall in notrump shows the minor suits.

4) Jumps show two suiters as follows:

   a) A jump in diamonds shows diamonds and hearts.

   b) A jump in hearts shows hearts and clubs.

   c) A jump in spades shows spades and a minor suit. Advancer can bid notrump to ask which minor suit.

7. ROBINSON

This defense to a forcing club was developed by Kit Woolsey who named it for his long-time regular partner.

1) Double is strong, showing sixteen or more high card points.

2) One diamond shows either a red or black two suiter.

3) One heart shows either a major or minor two suiter.

4) One spade is natural and can be quite weak — destructive rather than constructive.

5) One notrump shows either clubs and hearts, or diamonds and spades.

6) All two level bids are natural one suiters.

8. CRASH

This conventional defense against a forcing club, developed by Kit Woolsey and Steve Robinson, is probably the most esoteric and, when used properly, the most effective defense that has been developed. Its effectiveness comes from the fact that bids are used to show combinations of two suits. However, since the two suits that are being shown are not known to the users of the forcing club, they are unable to Cuebid opposing suits when they have forward going hands.

The name is an acronym which stands for Color, RAnk, SHape. A double of the forcing club opening bid shows two suits of the same Color; an overcall of one diamond shows two suits of the same RAnk. Bids in the major suits are natural, and a bid of one notrump shows two suits of the same SHape.

Advancer's actions are dictated by the degree of fit he has for one of the two suits shown by the intruder's action, regardless of which pair of suits he holds. With only moderate values and 4-2-3-4, or 4-2-2-5 distribution, when the competitive call of double shows two suits of the same color, Advancer can do nothing but bid two diamonds. He should not wish to increase the level when he has a poor fit for the suits that he assumes have been shown. If the suits shown are actually the black suits, the intruder will correct to spades, and Advancer may be able to move forward with knowledge that a two-suited fit has been found. If Advancer has length in a suit of each color, he can jump preemptively to the level at which he is content to play. If, for example, he is four-four or longer in clubs and hearts, when his partner shows two suits of the same Color, Advancer may be able to jump to three clubs. This should not be mistaken as showing a club suit. When the intruder holds red suits, he corrects to three diamonds. When the correction shows that the intruder holds both red suits, Advancer corrects once more to his longer heart holding.

The same concept applies when the intruder shows two suits of the same RAnk (either both majors or both minors), or two suits of the same SHape (either both rounded suits or both pointed suits). When the Advancer has a guaranteed fit for one of the unknown suits that have been shown because he holds length in one suit of each pair, he can bid to the level he finds appropriate. He knows that partner will pass if one of the shown suits has been bid, or will correct when he holds the other pair, for which Advancer is prepared.

Modifications of this convention allow for transfers to keep the forcing club bidder on opening lead. In such modifications, when the intruder is next to bid immediately after the opening one club bid:

1) Double shows two suits of the same Color.
2) One diamond is a transfer to hearts.
3) One heart is a transfer to spades.
4) One spade shows two suits of the same RAnk.
5) One notrump shows two suits of the same SHape.
6) All immediate bids at any level are also transfers, with two, three or four clubs transferring to diamonds; two, three or four diamonds transferring to hearts; two, three or four hearts transferring to spades; and two, three or four spades transferring to clubs.

When the intruder enters the auction after a response of one diamond, instead of making transfer bids, his suit bids are natural so that the forcing club bidder remains on lead against a contract by the intruding side. After a one diamond response:

1) Double shows two suits of the same Color.
2) One heart and one spade are natural.
3) One notrump shows two suits of the same RAnk.
4) Two clubs shows two suits of the same SHape.
5) Bids in suits at higher levels are all natural.

Yet another revision allows the intruder to show a three suited hand. The bid in each auction directly beyond the bid which shows two suits of the same shape is used artificially to show a three-suiter. The Advancer can then call in his nearest four card (or possibly three card) holding. If that is a suit held by the intruder he can pass or raise. If that is the intruder's short suit, he bids the next suit available, allowing Advancer to pass or correct further.

When competitive bidders are able to master the intricacies of responding so they reach the proper level regardless of which pair of suits has been shown by the intruder, their ability to defend against the forcing club opening bid becomes extremely effective.

CHAPTER FOURTEEN
DEFENSES TO OPPONENTS' OPENING WEAK TWO BIDS

Showing a good two suited hand when an opponent has opened with a weak two bid should be something that any partnership can do. At this writing there are apparently three conventional approaches in use. We will present them in the order of their usefulness. It is our opinion, of course, but we will include the reasons which we believe will have the reader agree.

MICHAELS CUE BIDS AFTER OPPOSING WEAK TWO BIDS

Those who have not thought deeply about the need to have a defense to show two suits when an opponent has opened with a weak two bid probably use a Cue Bid for that purpose. They play Michaels because the rest of the world plays Michaels. They see no reason to delve further to find an answer to the problems presented when a weak two bid is opened by an opponent. Let us look at what the problem is and see why Michaels does not solve it.

When the weak two bid is in a major suit, the Cue Bid will show the other major and an undisclosed minor suit. When the Advancer has no fit for the other major suit, he will need to know which minor suit the Cue Bidder holds. To find out, he must bid three notrump.

How can the Michaels bidder tell whether his partner is trying to find out what his second suit is, or whether he truly has some values and a stopper in the suit of the weak two bid and wants to play three notrump? The answer — he cannot.

And what if the Responder, after hearing the weak two bid and the Cue Bid, preemptively raises to game. When the Advancer needs to know the second suit he will have to bid four notrump.

Should that be to play? Or should it be Blackwood? Or should it seek the second suit held by the Cue Bidder?

If it does ask the Cue Bidder to name his second suit, how does the Advancer guess whether to play at the five level or the six level?

When the weak two bid is in diamonds, things are easier. The Michaels call of three diamonds shows two known suits, the majors. Now the Advancer can choose a major to bid at the three level or jump to the four level.

But once again, what happens when the Responder gets into the act and raises after the cue bid? When the Advancer bids the major suit of his choice at the four level, neither partner will have a clue as to the level at which they should play.

The Cue Bidder will not know whether the Advancer has stretched to bid at the four level, or whether he has extra values which might produce a slam. And the Advancer will have little option but to simply bid at the four level with extra values, since the Cue Bidder might have stretched to bid due to his shape.

If you are starting to understand why Michaels does not work against weak two bids, that is because you have been paying attention. Yet, in any given session of tournament bridge, the percentage of entrants who have never thought about the problem and as a result, still play Michaels, would run at about ninety.

But wait! There's more! What happens when after the opening weak two bid the ready intruder holds a wonderful hand with a source of tricks and no stopper in the suit of the weak two bid? He can overcall or he can double. But he cannot let his partner know that all he needs to make a game in notrump is to find a stopper in the suit of the weak two bid in his partner's hand.

If he is lucky, when he elects to either double or overcall, the Advancer might realize that all that is needed is a stopper in the suit of the weak two bid, and bid three notrump. That would be wonderful, but will he take that action when he holds the king of the weak two bid suit and no other high cards?

We will end this discussion by simply stating that against weak two bids, Michaels has virtually no value, despite the fact that the majority of tournament players have never discovered this fact. They have never even thought about the problem, and woodenly use Michaels just because that is what they do to show two suits against an opposing opening bid. If you did not start this book in the middle, perhaps you have already given up the use of Michaels altogether.

SCHLEIFER

There is a defense to show two suited hands against weak two bids which is widely used at the expert level. It goes a long way toward solving the problem and does have considerable merit. We understand that the originator was the late, great Meyer Schleifer. Whether or not that is true is not significant. Just as Sam Stayman will forever receive credit for the Rapee convention, Schleifer may be credited falsely with someone else's idea. But what harm can that do if it is so?

The Schleifer convention to be used against an opposing weak two bid assumes that the weak two bid will usually be in a major suit. It uses a jump overcall in a minor suit to show that minor and the unbid major. The jump overcaller will have a good hand and at least five-five distribution in the two suits he has shown.

There is no defintion when the opening bid is in diamonds. If a jump in clubs shows clubs and a major suit, which major suit does it show? If a jump in hearts shows both major suits, how does the bidder show the other minor suit and one of the majors? Don't worry because few pairs use weak two bids in diamonds.

Aside from the two diamond problem, the fact that a Cue Bid is available to help the bidding side find three notrump is a blessing. If the intruder Cue Bids the suit of the weak two bid, he announces that he has a good hand with a source of tricks, and seeks a stopper in the suit of the weak two bid. This often works well.

When the Cue Bid faces an Advancer who does not hold a stopper in the suit of the weak two bid, he announces that fact by bidding in the cheapest available suit. After an auction of: 2♥ -

3♥ - Pass - 3♠, the Advancer has simply said that he does not hold a stopper in hearts, not that he has a desire to play in spades. When the Cue Bidder holds a solid seven card spade suit (truly a possibility), he raises the temporizing call to game. Otherwise, he corrects to the suit which is his real source of tricks.

When the intruder hears an opposing weak two bid and has a two suiter with both minor suits, things get sticky. When he wishes to get into the auction and show his two suiter, he has two possible actions to take. With a very good two suiter, he makes a jump Cue Bid at the four level, which requires the Advancer to name a minor suit at the five level.

With a hand which is not so good, the intruder warns the Advancer about the nature of his hand by instead jumping to four notrump. This announces a hand with both minor suits, but suggests that there is some doubt that the contract will make. When the Advancer holds a hand with shortness in both minor suits, this prophecy often is fulfilled quite soundly.

We note that although this convention does have a chance to get the intruding side to three notrump (and does work when the Advancer has a fit for one of the suits shown by the Cue Bidder or Overcaller), there are inherent weaknesses in the approach.

Despite the weaknesses that have been noted, this convention is used by the majority of the remaining ten percent who do not use Michaels. Not only do they use it, but they also misname it. They call it by the name of the convention which actually does work in most instances. They insist that they are using Roman Jumps.

It is for this reason that when an experienced pair is filling out a convention card and one of the two suggests Roman Jumps against opposing weak two bids, it is imperative that one who understands the difference between that convention and Schleifer speak up. He needs to be sure of what the agreement being sought actually is. Those who know the terminology and the difference between approaches will understand the need to use the best available tool, and will agree to play Roman Jumps with an understanding of what they actually are.

ROMAN JUMPS

We have finally arrived. The defense against weak two bids to show two suited hands which truly works is Roman Jumps. Let us summarize the entire approach.

A cue bid of the weak two bid suit asks for a stopper in that suit. The Cue Bidder will have a good hand, usually with a long solid (or semi-solid) suit which will be a source of tricks. When the Advancer holds a stopper in the suit of the weak two bid, he bids three notrump without worry, for the Cue Bidder will hold many tricks and simply lack a stopper in the suit of the opponents.

When the Advancer does not hold a stopper, he bids in the cheapest suit, and allows the Cue Bidder to correct to his long suit. As in the example previously mentioned: 2♥ - 3♥ - Pass - 3♠, does not show a spade suit. This writer has, in fact, declared four spades in this exact auction when he bid his doubleton and was raised by the Cue Bidder who held seven solid spades.

Jump overcalls show specific two suited hands. The jump overcaller will hold the suit in which he has jumped, and the next available suit, excluding the suit of the opening weak two bid. After an opening bid of two hearts, for example, these are the suits shown by a jump overcall:

1) A jump to three spades shows spades and clubs.
2) A jump to four clubs shows clubs and diamonds.
3) A jump to four diamonds shows diamonds and spades.

Note that there is no ambiguity regarding the suits that the jump overcall has shown. Note also that it is possible for the Advancer to get out cheaply in a minor suit when he holds a poor hand and the jump overcall shows both minor suits.

The Roman Jump overcall promises at least five-five distribution with a good hand. It is rare when the jump overcaller holds the hand he has promised, and his side will be too high or without a fit in which to play. Of the tools to be used to show two suited hands when an opponent has opened with a weak two bid, this is the one that works. We recommend it highly.

CHAPTER FIFTEEN
A DAY AT THE OFFICE

We began in Chapter One by culling hand record printouts and finding hands that we believe cannot be bid easily when current methods are used. We showed thirty such hands in Chapter One, and then introduced methods which could be used to bid those hands. In Chapter Six we brought back those thirty hands and showed how each of them could be described no matter what opposing opening bid had been made.

In this last Chapter, we are going to take hands from one day at a Regional tournament, selected at random. The hands that will be used were played at the Sacramento Regional on May 30, 1995. We will present each hand from the two hand record sheets which relate to the subjects we have covered and identify it. Then we will put it into a scenario which might occur, and in which you might be faced with the problem of how to express that hand to your partner.

In the two hand printouts from a single day, we found more than fifty hands which might be held when the opposition created a problem of description after an opposing opening bid. Having presented methods to cope with situations which might occur, we will deal with problems that might arise if you held the particular hand that has been shown.

We emphasize again that we have not created these hands. They were dealt by computer and used at a sanctioned ACBL Regional tournament. What we have done is to give you each hand, and create a situation in which you would probably be unable to express to your partner what you are looking at without proper tools. We hope that this set of exercises will convince you (if you have not already been convinced) that currently available tools which are being used by the masses are inferior. We hope you agree that the tools we have advocated in these pages will more readily solve the bidding problems that you might face at any given time.

1. Board 1 North. You hold:

♠ AQJ62
♥ A9873
♦ J
♣ AQ

Against an opposing opening bid of two diamonds, jump to three hearts. You hold an excellent two suiter. If you overcalled in spades, you might play there when you were cold for a slam in hearts. Double might work, but if partner passed for penalties you probably would not score as well as if your side declared at an appropriate contract.

Against a minor suit opening bid at the one level, the field might use Michaels, and then jump to game in the major suit selected by the Advancer. This could work out. We would double, then Cue Bid after partner selected a major suit. If he selected the other minor suit, we would again Cue Bid to suggest that he select from among his three card major suit holdings.

2. Board 1 West. You hold:

♠ 10
♥ KJ1062
♦ AQ5
♣ KJ32

When the opponents open with one of either minor suit, a simple overcall in hearts will do for a start. When they open with one spade, overcall by bidding two hearts so that you will be able to find a five-three fit in hearts if it exists. At your next turn, if partner has been silent, you can double to show support for both unbid suits. If you double at your first turn, you will almost never get to hearts when you have a five-three fit, or even when partner holds honor doubleton.

3. Board 2 North. You hold:

$\spadesuit$ AKQJ5
$\heartsuit$ K8
$\diamondsuit$ K10832
$\clubsuit$ J

When the opening bid against you is one club, bid two clubs, a Top and Bottom Cue Bid. Your partner will usually bid diamonds when he holds an ordinary hand, for your Cue Bid suggests that diamonds are long or stronger than spades in your hand. However, your followup will be a voluntary bid in spades, which will show that you have a very strong hand with at least five-five distribution.

When the opening bid against you is two hearts, jump to four diamonds. This shows a very good hand with at least five-five in diamonds and spades.

4. Board 3 North. You hold:

$\spadesuit$ AKQ42
$\heartsuit$ AK963
$\diamondsuit$ —
$\clubsuit$ AK2

When your hand is this powerful, you will not expect an opponent to be able to open the bidding against you. The tools discussed here will not be of much value when an opponent does open the bidding, nor would tools which are currently standard, with the exception of Michaels.

We suggest a Cue bid when either minor suit is opened, probably to be followed by a repeat of that Cue Bid. If partner does select a major suit, just raise him to the six level. If he shows hearts, check for the heart queen, and if he holds it, raise to seven.

5. Board 4 South. You hold:

♠ J6432
♥ 9
♦ 1097654
♣ 3

What a dog!! But it does have wonderful distribution. When you are not vulnerable versus vulnerable, compete with the Unusual Notrump if the action sounds right and you can show these two suits. In most auctions, you will do best to remain silent and let the opponents run afoul of the unexpected distribution.

6. Board 6 North. You hold:

♠ Q872
♥ 532
♦ AJ1094
♣ K

When the vulnerability is favorable and the opening bid is one heart, feel free to double if you are a passed hand. Partner will expect three suits, but you have equal level correction available. When the opening bid is one club, you have a problem. A Top and Bottom Cue Bid would express your better suits, but if partner has length in hearts he might be dissuaded from bidding them, and you would have a nice dummy at a heart contract.

7. Board 7 North. You hold:

♠ 10
♥ AQJ642
♦ 97
♣ AQJ8

This is certainly a fine hand with excellent offensive potential. However, do not get caught up with systemic devices here.

Against any opening bid, including two spades, bid hearts. Your clubs are a nice side holding, but your primary concern is to show your good heart suit. Given the later opportunity to show clubs, you should consider that possibility, but only if partner understands how good your heart suit is first.

8. Board 7 South. You hold:

♠ AJ986
♥ —
♦ QJ862
♣ K43

If your five card suits were interchanged, you might consider a Top and Bottom call after an opening bid of one club, but not with your actual hand which has better spades than diamonds. After any opening bid, overcall in spades and reserve options for later in the auction. Given the chance to urge partner into the auction at your second turn, you must decide between bidding diamonds and doubling to show both of the unbid suits. The length disparity should have you suggest diamonds rather than show both suits.

9. Board 9 East. You hold:

♠ A1086
♥ A83
♦ K
♣ Q10732

Against an opening bid of one diamond you can make a takeout double. When the opening bid is one heart, make a Top and Bottom Cue Bid to show your clubs and spades.

10. Board 11 West. You hold:

♠ A1054
♥ A104
♦ 8
♣ KQJ53

Almost deja vu. You have the same solutions as with the previous problem, except that your hand is much better.

11. Board 11 South. You hold:

♠ 97
♥ QJ9753
♦ AKQJ
♣ A

Another very nice hand. Don't make the error of only overcalling in hearts when they open the bidding in a black suit against you. This hand is certainly good enough for a Type 2 takeout double. Double first, then bid hearts. You need little but a fit to make a game. When the opening bid has been one spade and the Advancer bids clubs after your takeout double, your rebid of two hearts will show your good hand. The correction is not to the lower ranking of the two remaining suits which would be equal level correction. When the opening bid is in clubs and partner bids spades in response to your double, your correction to hearts shows your excellent hand. If after you correct clubs to hearts the opponents compete in spades again (unlikely), introduce your diamond suit as well.

12. Board 13 North. You hold:

♠ J9652
♥ —
♦ AKJ543
♣ K4

Against an opening bid of one club, you are delighted that you are playing Top and Bottom Cue Bids. When the opening bid is one heart, make a Type four takeout double and correct from clubs to diamonds to show this good offensive hand.

13. Board 14 South. You hold:

♠ A8
♥ J6
♦ A952
♣ AJ1082

Against an opening major suit bid, don't go bonkers with an Unusual Notrump call. Just overcall in clubs. When Responder raises to the two level and you are in the balance position at the two level, bid two notrump if the vulnerability is right. This will show that in addition to clubs you also hold shorter diamonds.

14. Board 15 North. You hold:

♠ KQJ874
♥ K
♦ K1064
♣ 63

Don't let the second suit get you excited. Compete in spades against opposing bidding, but don't introduce diamonds unless you have the chance to bid spades twice. The fine quality of your long suit should make it a good trump suit unless partner is void and has lots of diamonds. Only when that possibility exists should your second suit be given consideration.

15. Board 15 West. You hold:

♠ A5
♥ A762
♦ 98752
♣ Q2

You have the shape to compete, but don't get carried away. Your values are misplaced and your longest suit is headless. If the opening bid is one club, you can bid two diamonds to show diamonds and hearts, but you should consider this action only if the situation is right. Not vul versus vul, or if in desperate need of a swing, use your jump overcall, but don't be proud of it.

16. Board 18 North. You hold:

♠ K97
♥ AQJ10963
♦ J
♣ AQ

Here is a hand that is truly worth a Type two takeout double. No matter what the opening bid against you is, an overcall in hearts does not do justice to this hand. It needs almost nothing but a marginal fit and the ace of spades to have a shot at a slam. Double, then show your heart suit, but be careful not to make an equal level correction call.

17. Board 18 West. You hold:

♠ A84
♥ K872
♦ A9764
♣ 6

This is a marginal hand with which to compete, but under the right circumstances you might want to do just that. A passed hand takeout double of an opening bid of one club is fine. A passed hand takeout double of an opening bid of one spade will also work, because you have equal level correction at your disposal.

18. Board 20 North. You hold:

♠ A5
♥ AKQJ93
♦ 75
♣ A106

Against an opening bid of one in either other suit, make a Type two takeout double, then show your good heart suit. When the opening bid is two diamonds, Cue Bid to see if partner holds any useful diamond cards. If he does not, when you show your heart suit you will have described an excellent hand with a source of tricks in hearts.

19. Board 20 South. You hold:

♠ KJ9842
♥ 5
♦ A1096
♣ K7

The excellent shape and good spot cards in this hand give you license to compete. You will probably not have a chance to show your second suit, but be vigorous if the auction stops early.

20. Board 22 North. You hold:

♠ 32
♥ AK62
♦ K6
♣ Q6542

When the opening bid against you is one spade, make a Top and Bottom Cue Bid. When the opening bid is one diamond, bid three clubs to show your two suits. When the opening bid is one club, overcall one heart.

21. Board 26 East. You hold:

♠ K
♥ 8
♦ 86532
♣ AK8753

After a major suit opening bid, do not use the Unusual Notrump. Your defensive potential is great, so overcall two clubs on your good suit. If the Responder raises and you are in the balance position at the two level, bid two notrump to show that you have diamonds as well as clubs.

22. Board 27 North. You hold:

♠ A9
♥ AJ
♦ K863
♣ A8754

Nobody says you have to like the bids that you may have to make. As first to speak, one notrump is probably better than any alternative. When the opposition opens with one of a major suit, nothing appeals because of the bad suit textures. Overcalling in clubs and later bidding notrump to show a shorter diamond suit might work, but again the quality of the suits should dissuade you. We recommend a special convention created by our friend Jerry Helms, called WIRDI. "Whatever Is Right Do It." Make your best guess.

23. Board 29 West. You hold:

♠ AK8765
♥ Q96
♦ A
♣ K97

This hand is dangerously misleading. If you just look at suit lengths and count points, you might make a takeout double, then bid spades. This hand is not good enough for that action. The suit is empty after the top two honors, and the diamond ace is not a working card. Singleton aces are not worth the extra points assigned when the would be point counter starts with four for the ace, then adds two for the singleton. When an ace is singleton, don't add points; subtract a point for the fact that the ace is not helping create additional tricks.

24. Board 34 East. You hold:

♠ Q104
♥ A972
♦ AQJ32
♣ 2

Against an opening bid of either one club or one spade, you can make a takeout double. Neither action is picture perfect. When the opening bid has been in clubs and partner bids spades in response to your double, you would like to have another card in the suit. When the opening bid has been in spades, if partner bids clubs you can use equal level correction, but you should not be very proud of your soft spade queen.

25. Board 35 North. You hold:

> ♠ AQ1075
> ♥ A7
> ♦ 8
> ♣ J8643

Don't get convention happy with this one. Overcall in spades and don't mention clubs unless strange things happen. If partner doesn't fit spades, then you might try clubs at the three level when given a chance, but it will be a real gamble.

SECOND SESSION HANDS

26. Board 1 South. You hold:

> ♠ QJ95
> ♥ 2
> ♦ Q6432
> ♣ J93

When your partner has passed and you are not vulnerable, you might try a Top and Bottom Cue Bid if your right hand opponent opens the bidding with one club. This is suggested at match points only. When partner holds a fit with either spades or diamonds and can preemptively raise either suit that you have shown, the opponents will not have an easy time getting to their best level in one of their fits.

27. Board 3 North. You hold:

> ♠ KQ862
> ♥ 2
> ♦ KQJ104
> ♣ 76

This hand does pose some problems. You would like to show

both suits, but spades are nearly as good as diamonds and equal in length. So a Top and Bottom Cue Bid would not give a good description after an opposing opening bid of one club. If you overcall in spades, you might not be able to get your good diamond suit into the picture.

Although excellent offensively, this hand has little potential defense since both possible defensive tricks are second round tricks which could be negated by a singleton in an opponent's hand.

Perhaps the best description would be possible after clubs and hearts have both been bid by the opposition. An Unusual No-trump call will show your good shape and offensive potential while downplaying the questionable defensive prowess of this hand.

28. Board 6 South. You hold:

♠ 8
♥ AK102
♦ 1032
♣ AQ984

A perfect hand for our systemic tools. When the opening bid is one spade you can double for takeout, but to emphasize your real suits you can make a Top and Bottom Cue Bid. When the opening bid is one diamond, you can jump to three clubs to show clubs and hearts with longer clubs. When the opening bid is either one club or one heart, you can overcall in the other of those two suits.

29. Board 7 North. You hold:

> ♠ 9865
> ♥ A
> ♦ KQ1065
> ♣ Q97

Against an opening bid of one club, a Top and Bottom Cue Bid allows you to show your nice diamond suit and still suggest spades in case partner has length in that suit. Those who do not have the use of our tools will overcall in diamonds and most likely lose a spade fit whenever one exists.

30. Board 8 South. You hold:

> ♠ 6
> ♥ A2
> ♦ KQ975
> ♣ AQJ95

This hand is almost good enough to use the Unusual Notrump against a major suit opening bid, then bid again to invite a slam. We suggest instead that you overcall in diamonds, then bid clubs at your next turn to show a good minor two-suiter.

31. Board 9 East. You hold:

> ♠ KJ73
> ♥ K10
> ♦ KQ872
> ♣ A5

Another hand which can be expressed by a Top and Bottom Cue Bid when the opening bid against you is one club. When they open one heart, make a takeout double and correct to diamonds if partner responds to your takeout double in clubs.

32. Board 10 South. You hold:

♠ KJ86
♥ KJ962
♦ K6
♣ A8

Against a minor suit opening bid, don't make the error of overcalling one notrump. Make a takeout double and use equal level correction if you have to.

33. Board 12 East. You hold:

♠ 109763
♥ J
♦ A9742
♣ 32

When not vulnerable, you might want to show your two suits after the opponents have bid clubs and hearts. With good shape and only one defensive trick, you can use the Unusual Notrump. If you have passed, bid one notrump. If you have not passed, jump to two notrump.

34. Board 14 East. You hold:

♠ Q3
♥ A62
♦ AJ9
♣ AKQ98

When the opening bid has been one club, diamond, or heart, and there have been two passes, jump to two notrump in the balance position to show this excellent hand. When the opening bid was one spade, make a takeout double instead.

35. Board 14 South. You hold:

♠ J10965
♥ 84
♦ K87643
♣ —

If you are not vulnerable and your partner has passed, you might bluff a show of strength against an opening bid of one club by making a Top and Bottom Cue Bid. When your opponents have bid clubs and hearts, use the Unusual Notrump. Preempt as much as you feel necessary. A jump to four notrump at this vulnerability has merit.

36. Board 17 North. You hold:

♠ 9875
♥ A9
♦ AJ1073
♣ 106

When the opponent at your right opens with one club, the world will overcall one diamond. You can make a Top and Bottom Cue Bid, so that the spade suit will not be lost if partner has length there.

37. Board 17 West. You hold:

♠ KQJ42
♥ 6
♦ 94
♣ AQJ42

It is very close as to whether this hand is good enough to make a Top and Bottom Cue bid against a red suit opening bid, then bid spades at your next turn. Your decision to do this will be prompted by tactical considerations. If you are willing to be pushy to try for a good result, do it.

38. Board 18 South. You hold:

♠ K864
♥ 3
♦ QJ10852
♣ K3

You would love to hear your right hand opponent open by bidding one club. You have an excellent Top and Bottom Cue Bid. If your spades and hearts were interchanged, you would jump to two diamonds to show that particular hand.

39. Board 20 North. You hold:

♠ 106542
♥ K
♦ A
♣ QJ10532

How sweet to be able to Cue Bid against an opening bid in either red suit. Michaels users can do so after an opening bid of one heart, but they are stuck when the opening bid is one diamond.

40. Board 20 East. You hold:

♠ A
♥ A1072
♦ K108764
♣ A9

Against an opening bid of one spade, you can make a takeout double, and if partner bids clubs you have an easy correction to diamonds. When the opening bid is one club, your jump to two diamonds describes this hand to a tee.

41. Board 21 South. You hold:

♠ KQ52
♥ KQ1097
♦ 1042
♣ 2

If you are brave enough to make a takeout double with this hand after an opening bid of one diamond, when the Advancer bids clubs you can make an equal level correction to hearts. If you overcall in hearts, the spade suit might get lost. On the other hand, your takeout double will cause your partner to believe that you have better defensive strength, which could lead to problems. The takeout double is easier if your partner has passed.

42. Board 23 East. You hold:

♠ 2
♥ J9863
♦ A9
♣ KJ864

Another bread and butter hand for our methods. Against an opening bid of one spade, make a Top and Bottom Cue Bid. Against an opening bid of one diamond, jump to three clubs.

43. Board 23 South. You hold:

♠ AK10976
♥ —
♦ Q108762
♣ 3

When the opening bid is one heart, emphasize spades by overcalling, but plan to bid diamonds once, or even twice, later in the auction. If the opening bid is one club, make a Top and Bottom Cue Bid, then bid spades voluntarily. Although you do not have the values that are normally expected for this auction, your distribution will cause you to compete to a very high level.

44. Board 24 North. You hold:

♠ K
♥ KQ63
♦ AKQ83
♣ J94

When the opponents open with one club, jump to two diamonds to show your red suits and emphasize diamonds. When the opening bid is one spade, make a takeout double. When the opening bid is one diamond (quite unlikely) overcall in hearts.

45. Board 28 East. You hold:

♠ 10965
♥ —
♦ A9432
♣ A972

Against an opening bid of one heart, you can make a takeout double. Your shape is classic and you do have two defensive tricks. When the opening bid is one club, you can make a Top and Bottom Cue Bid to show your diamonds and spades.

46. Board 28 South. You hold:

♠ KQ83
♥ K10753
♦ Q106
♣ K

When the opening bid on your right is one club anyone can make a takeout double. When the opening bid is one diamond, you can still make a takeout double and use equal level correction.

47. Board 30 North. You hold:

> ♠ —
> ♥ A963
> ♦ J83
> ♣ KJ10752

After an opening bid of one diamond, jump to three clubs to show your six-four in clubs and hearts. When the opening bid is one spade, a Top and Bottom Cue Bid might lose a diamond fit in partner's hand, but you hardly have the values to make a takeout double.

48. Board 33 East. You hold:

> ♠ 42
> ♥ Q762
> ♦ 65
> ♣ K9642

Again we observe a case of almost no values, but a hand with the shape to compete in the right situation. If not vulnerable and partner is a passed hand, either a Top and Bottom Cue Bid against an opening bid of one spade, or a jump to three clubs after an opening bid of one diamond might create a problem for your opponents. Here, your tools will not be used constructively, but for the purpose of impeding your opponents who surely have a game, and probably have a slam.

49. Board 34 North. You hold:

♠ A3
♥ 32
♦ K
♣ AKQJ10764

This is a very reasonable hand with which to make a Cue Bid after an opposing opening bid of two hearts. If partner holds a heart stopper you surely want to suggest three notrump. If partner bids three spades over your Cue Bid of three hearts (remember that this does not show spades, but simply denies a heart stopper), you will correct to four clubs.

50. Board 35 South. You hold:

♠ KJ95
♥ K8
♦ K3
♣ A10982

We close with another classic. When the opponents open in either red suit, your Top and Bottom Cue Bid will give a reasonable picture of your hand to your partner. He will expect clubs and spades with longer or stronger clubs.

* *

If we had created hands to illustrate the use of all of the tools which have been discussed in this book, we could have done a more thorough job of covering the territory. As in any two sessions of tournament bridge, one does not expect situations to come up which will tax all of the available conventions agreed by any one pair.

The fact that from these two pages of hands we covered several, but not all of the methods presented herein should convince the skeptic that the hands actually came from the sources to which we have attributed them. If you have doubts and would like proof, send a FAX to (702) 362-0686, and we will return a FAX showing the actual printed hand sources for your inspection.

50 HIGHLY-RECOMMENDED TITLES

CALL TOLL FREE 1-800-274-2221
IN THE U.S. & CANADA TO ORDER ANY OF
THEM OR TO REQUEST OUR
FULL-COLOR 64 PAGE CATALOG OF
ALL BRIDGE BOOKS IN PRINT,
SUPPLIES AND GIFTS.

FOR BEGINNERS
#0300 Future Champions' Bridge Series 9.95
#2130 Kantar-Introduction to Declarer's Play 10.00
#2135 Kantar-Introduction to Defender's Play 10.00
#0101 Stewart-Baron-The Bridge Book 1 .... 9.95
#1121 Silverman-Elementary Bridge
            Five Card Major Student Text 4.95
#0660 Penick-Beginning Bridge Complete 9.95
#0661 Penick-Beginning Bridge Quizzes 6.95
#3230 Lampert-Fun Way to Serious Bridge 10.00

FOR ADVANCED PLAYERS
#2250 Reese-Master Play 5.95
#1420 Klinger-Modern Losing Trick Count 14.95
#2240 Love-Bridge Squeezes Complete 7.95
#0103 Stewart-Baron-The Bridge Book 3 .... 9.95
#0740 Woolsey-Matchpoints 14.95
#0741 Woolsey-Partnership Defense 12.95
#1702 Bergen-Competitive Auctions 9.95
#0636 Lawrence-Falsecards 9.95

BIDDING — 2 OVER 1 GAME FORCE
#4750 Bruno & Hardy-Two-Over-One Game Force:
            An Introduction 9.95
#1750 Hardy-Two-Over-One Game Force 14.95
#1790 Lawrence-Workbook on the Two Over One System 11.95
#4525 Lawrence-Bidding Quizzes Book 1 .... 13.95

Prices subject to change without notice.

DEFENSE
#0520 Blackwood-Complete Book of Opening Leads........... 17.95
#3030 Ewen-Opening Leads 15.95
#0104 Stewart-Baron-The Bridge Book 4 .... 7.95
#0631 Lawrence-Dynamic Defense... 11.95
#1200 Woolsey-Modern Defensive Signalling 4.95

FOR INTERMEDIATE PLAYERS
#2120 Kantar-Complete Defensive Bridge 20.00
#3015 Root-Commonsense Bidding 15.00
#0630 Lawrence-Card Combinations 12.95
#0102 Stewart-Baron-The Bridge Book 2 .... 9.95
#1122 Silverman-Intermediate Bridge Five
    Card Major Student Text 4.95
#0575 Lampert-The Fun Way to Advanced Bridge 11.95
#0633 Lawrence-How to Read Your Opponents' Cards 11.95
#3672 Truscott-Bid Better, Play Better 12.95
#1765 Lawrence-Judgment at Bridge 9.95

PLAY OF THE HAND
#2150 Kantar-Test your Bridge Play, Vol. 1 .... 10.00
#3675 Watson-Watson's Classic Book on
    the Play of the Hand... 15.00
#1932 Mollo-Gardener-Card Play Technique 12.95
#3009 Root-How to Play a Bridge Hand 15.00
#1124 Silverman-Play of the Hand as
    Declarer and Defender 4.95
#2175 Truscott-Winning Declarer Play 10.00
#3803 Sydnor-Bridge Made Easy Book 3 .... 8.00

CONVENTIONS
#2115 Kantar-Bridge Conventions.. 10.00
#0610 Kearse-Bridge Conventions Complete 29.95
#3011 Root-Pavlicek-Modern Bridge Conventions 15.00
#0240 Championship Bridge Series (All 36) 25.95

DUPLICATE STRATEGY
#1600 Klinger-50 Winning Duplicate Tips 12.95
#2260 Sheinwold-Duplicate Bridge 4.95

FOR ALL PLAYERS
#3889 Darvas & de V. Hart-Right Through The Pack 14.95
#0790 Simon: Why You Lose at Bridge 11.95
#4850 Encyclopedia of Bridge, Official (ACBL) 39.95

Andersen THE LEBENSOHL CONVENTION COMPLETE .... $ 6.95
Baron THE BRIDGE PLAYER'S DICTIONARY $19.95
Bergen BETTER BIDDING WITH BERGEN,
     Vol. I, Uncontested Auctions $11.95
Bergen BETTER BIDDING WITH BERGEN,
     Vol. II, Competitive Auctions .... $ 9.95
Blackwood COMPLETE BOOK OF OPENING LEADS $17.95
Blackwood-Hanson PLAY FUNDAMENTALS .... $ 6.95
Boeder THINKING ABOUT IMPS $12.95
Bruno-Hardy 2 OVER 1 GAME FORCE: AN INTRODUCTION .... $ 9.95
Darvas & De V. Hart RIGHT THROUGH THE PACK $14.95
DeSerpa THE MEXICAN CONTRACT .... $ 5.95
Eber & Freeman HAVE I GOT A STORY FOR YOU .... $ 7.95
Feldheim FIVE CARD MAJOR BIDDING IN
     CONTRACT BRIDGE $12.95
Flannery THE FLANNERY 2 DIAMOND OPENING .... $ 7.95
Goldman ACES SCIENTIFIC .... $ 9.95
Goldman WINNERS AND LOSERS AT THE
     BRIDGE TABLE .... $ 3.95
Groner DUPLICATE BRIDGE DIRECTION $14.95
Hardy
     COMPETITIVE BIDDING WITH 2-SUITED HANDS .... $ 9.95
     TWO-OVER-ONE GAME FORCE $14.95
     TWO-OVER-ONE GAME FORCE QUIZ BOOK $11.95
Harris BRIDGE DIRECTOR'S COMPANION (3rd Edition) $19.95
Kay COMPLETE BOOK OF DUPLICATE BRIDGE $14.95
Kearse BRIDGE CONVENTIONS COMPLETE $29.95
Kelsey THE TRICKY GAME $11.95
Lampert THE FUN WAY TO ADVANCED BRIDGE $11.95
Lawrence
     CARD COMBINATIONS $12.95
     COMPLETE BOOK ON BALANCING $11.95
     COMPLETE BOOK ON OVERCALLS $11.95
     DYNAMIC DEFENSE $11.95
     FALSECARDS .... $ 9.95
     HAND EVALUATION $11.95
     HOW TO READ YOUR OPPONENTS' CARDS $11.95
     JUDGMENT AT BRIDGE .... $ 9.95
     PARTNERSHIP UNDERSTANDINGS .... $ 5.95
     PLAY BRIDGE WITH MIKE LAWRENCE $11.95
     PLAY SWISS TEAMS WITH MIKE LAWRENCE .... $ 9.95
     WORKBOOK ON THE TWO OVER ONE SYSTEM $11.95

Lawrence & Hanson WINNING BRIDGE INTANGIBLES .... $ 4.95
Lipkin INVITATION TO ANNIHILATION .... $ 8.95
Michaels & Cohen 4-3-2-1 MANUAL .... $ 4.95
Penick BEGINNING BRIDGE COMPLETE .... $ 9.95
Penick BEGINNING BRIDGE QUIZZES .... $ 6.95
Robinson WASHINGTON STANDARD $19.95
Rosenkranz
     BRIDGE: THE BIDDER'S GAME $12.95
     TIPS FOR TOPS .... $ 9.95
     MORE TIPS FOR TOPS .... $ 9.95
     TRUMP LEADS .... $ 7.95
     OUR MAN GODFREY $10.95
Rosenkranz & Alder BID TO WIN, PLAY FOR PLEASURE $11.95
Rosenkranz & Truscott BIDDING ON TARGET $10.95
Silverman
     ELEMENTARY BRIDGE FIVE CARD MAJOR STUDENT TEXT .... $ 4.95
     INTERMEDIATE BRIDGE FIVE CARD MAJOR STUDENT TEXT .... $ 4.95
     ADVANCED & DUPLICATE BRIDGE STUDENT TEXT .... $ 4.95
     PLAY OF THE HAND AS DECLARER
     & DEFENDER STUDENT TEXT .... $ 4.95
Simon
     CUT FOR PARTNERS .... $ 9.95
     WHY YOU LOSE AT BRIDGE $11.95
Stewart & Baron
     THE BRIDGE BOOK, Vol. 1, Beginning .... $ 9.95
     THE BRIDGE BOOK, Vol. 2, Intermediate .... $ 9.95
     THE BRIDGE BOOK, Vol. 3, Advanced .... $ 9.95
     THE BRIDGE BOOK, Vol. 4, Defense .... $ 7.95
Truscott BID BETTER, PLAY BETTER $12.95
Von Elsner
     EVERYTHING'S JAKE WITH ME .... $ 5.95
     THE BEST OF JAKE WINKMAN .... $ 5.95
Wei PRECISION BIDDING SYSTEM .... $ 7.95
Woolsey
     MATCHPOINTS $14.95
     MODERN DEFENSIVE SIGNALLING .... $ 4.95
     PARTNERSHIP DEFENSE $12.95
World Bridge Federation APPEALS COMMITTEE DECISIONS
     from the 1994 NEC WORLD CHAMPIONSHIPS .... $ 9.95